GRAPHIC COMMUNICATIONS IN ARCHITECTURE

WILLIAM J. O'CONNELL

PROFESSOR OF ARCHITECTURE
UNIVERSITY OF ILLINOIS, URBANA

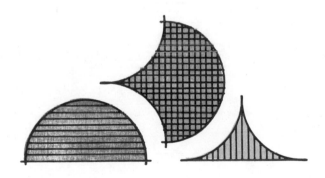

Fourth Printing

STIPES PUBLISHING COMPANY   CHAMPAIGN, ILLINOIS

GRAPHIC COMMUNICATIONS IN ARCHITECTURE

PREFACE

This book is concerned in general with graphic communications in architecture and the building industry and concerned in particular with architectural working drawings. The book has a threefold purpose: to explain architectural drawings to architecture and drafting students; to provide a usable format for architectural working drawings for architecture schools, drafting schools, and architectural and engineering firms; and to improve graphic communications in architecture and the building industry.

My earlier book, *Standard Format for Architectural Working Drawings,* published in 1966, provided a basis for this book. The format for architectural working drawings presented in the earlier book was in outline form. The format for architectural working drawings in this book is complete, but expandable, and is fully illustrated and explained.

To reduce drafting time and to facilitate a uniform approach to working drawings, material pertaining to the standard format for working drawings in this book is available commercially. See Appendix of book for information concerning purchase of material.

The rough draft of this book was read by many people. I thank those who reviewed the manuscript and offered criticism, in particular, Messrs. Robert A. Class, Thomas Nathan, and H. Leslie Simmons of the American Institute of Architects Production Office Procedures Committee; Professors George T. Clayton, Walter H. Lewis, Samuel T. Lanford, and Christopher A. Moyer of the Department of Architecture, University of Illinois, Urbana; and Architect James P. Warfield. Most of all, I thank my family. Without the help and encouragement of my wife, Dorothy, and without the prodding of our progeny, Dan, Jan, and Tom, the book could not have been written.

William J. O'Connell
Champaign, Illinois
March, 1972

GRAPHIC COMMUNICATIONS IN ARCHITECTURE

TABLE OF CONTENTS

| **1** | **GRAPHIC COMMUNICATIONS IN ARCHITECTURE** | **INTRODUCTION** | |

Construction fizzled on the Tower of Babel when Jehovah, angered by arrogant builders, caused tower workers to speak in different languages. The fiasco made headlines in the Bible. If it happened today, it would go unnoticed and unrecorded. Today, building construction is prolonged and made more costly, less durable, and less desirable because of poor graphic communications. The spectacle is overlooked by editors, ridiculed by building trades, tolerated by contractors, condoned by government, fostered by educators, instigated and perpetuated by design professions, financed by unaware owners, and permitted by Jehovah.

The building industry, even with the help of Jehovah, faces a task today far more difficult than that faced by the ill-fated Tower of Babel builders. New cities must be built and decaying ones renovated to accommodate expanding populations and economies. The colossal task cannot be accomplished with myriad graphic languages that plague the building industry.

The design professions, composed mainly of architects and engineers, prepare drawings during all phases of professional service. The ultimate purpose of the drawings is to transform a design concept into a building reality. The drawings are a means to an end, and, therefore, should be prepared efficiently and economically and should convey information concisely and unambiguously.

Architects and engineers communicate design concepts to themselves and clients with nontechnical schematic design drawings and outline specifications and with technical design development drawings and outline specifications. Since the number of people concerned with these documents is limited (owner, architect, engineers), the documents may be personalized. Architects and engineers communicate building design and construction to all members of the building industry with two legal technical documents: working drawings (that show what to do) and complementary final specifications (that tell how to do it). They concern all members of the building industry, and, therefore, should be formalized.

Presently each established design firm has its own unique graphic language for working drawings, and each newly formed firm is forced to devise its own. Some are good. Some are bad. They are all different. The proliferation of graphic languages, partly comprised of drafting standards and symbols and techniques for presenting drawings, increases confusion in the building industry resulting in higher construction costs, lower construction quality, and, ironically, lower professional profits.

Contrary to popular belief, the design professions spend most of their time on mundane matters. One-third of an architect's time on a typical construction project is spent preparing working drawings and another half is directly concerned with working drawings. Over 80% of an architect's time on most construction projects is affected by working drawings; yet, they are taken for granted by many architects (and engineers). There are few, if any, significant books or other publications on working drawings. Collegiate schools of architecture devote little or no time to the subject. The architectural profession has no required training program for novices to insure that they gain experience in working drawings. State registration boards do not examine architectural candidates in working drawings or require experience in their preparation. This inept system of inadequate publications, minimum or no education, chance professional experience, and unconcerned examinations produces costly, poorly prepared working drawings destined to confuse.

Professional journals are filled with articles on how to reduce working drawing production costs. Freehand techniques, cameras, drafting devices, office machines, and computers are featured. The articles and ideas are commendable, but they don't get to the heart of the problem. The design professions, in particular, and the building industry, in general, need a standard, flexible (permitting different dialects), and expandable graphic language (or notation system) to accommodate present and future design, construction, and contractual techniques. The building industry needs immediately a standard format for working drawings to complement the nationally known and accepted Construction Specifications Institute Format for Construction Specifications.

It should not be reasoned that since working

drawings today are esoteric contract documents between owner and contractor that all other lesser contract documents (based on preparation time) between owner and contractor are esoteric. The opposite is true. The American Institute of Architects publishes excellent standardized contract documents between owner and contractor; namely, forms of agreement between owner and contractor, general conditions of the contract for construction, and a change order form. The AIA also sponsors Production Systems for Architects and Engineers, Inc., that produces MASTERSPEC, a national automated specification system (that follows the CSI Format for Construction Specifications).

All design profession organizations should participate in the formation of a standard format for working drawings comprised of drafting standards and symbols and techniques for presenting drawings. Formats for all working drawing divisions, including architectural, structural, heating and ventilation, plumbing, electrical, civil, landscaping, and equipment working drawing divisions must be coordinated. Some standards, such as lettering heights, reference symbols, and material indications in section should be the same for all working drawing divisions. Other standards, such as lettering styles, sheet sizes and title blocks, and forms for schedules should be selective or optional.

The standard format must be pliable to accommodate small, medium, and large projects or offices. Although the standard format will necessarily curtail self-expression by draftsmen, it should not smother creativity or inhibit thinking. Most importantly, the format must not be devised solely to suit the convenience of the design professions. It must be formulated to satisfy the needs of all members of the building industry. It must be easily understood not only by the design professions but also by other members of the building industry who use working drawings.

A standard format for working drawings offers many advantages. It will reduce confusion in the building industry, allow detail drawings in files, catalogs, electronic film readers, and computers to be directly incorporated into working drawings, permit effective computerization of working drawings, reduce drafting mistakes, facilitate exchange of construction details, reduce busy work in schools and offices, expedite drafting and construction processes, facilitate development of building systems, reduce judgment errors, reduce construction mistakes, lower building construction costs, improve quality of building construction, increase professional profits, enable young professional firms to compete with older established professional firms, facilitate collaboration of design firms, enhance the image of design professions, enable architecture, engineering, and drafting schools to prepare students better for the design professions, and enable the design professions to serve the public better.

The design professions can reduce building construction costs and at the same time increase professional profits by devising and/or promoting a complete standard technical language for the building industry. The written half of the language is now administered by the Construction Specifications Institute. The graphic half of the language could be administered by a similar and complementary Construction Drawings Institute or by a Construction Drawings Council composed of representatives from design profession organizations and other concerned groups.

The standard format for architectural working drawings, illustrated and explained in succeeding pages, is a flexible format composed of office architectural drafting standards and symbols, project architectural drafting standards and symbols, and techniques for presenting architectural drawings. It can be used in schools by students and teachers and in offices by draftsmen and practitioners. More importantly, the format can be the beginning of a standard graphic language for the building industry, can be the foundation of a standard format for working drawings, and can be the catalyst for establishing a Construction Drawings Institute or a Construction Drawings Council.

With a standard graphic language for the building industry, composed in part of a standard format for working drawings, and a Construction Drawings Institute or Construction Drawings Council to administer it, architects, engineers, and builders would be sure that construction of new cities and renovation of old ones would not fizzle because of poor graphic communications.

Chapters 1 and 4 of this book are concerned with graphic communications in architecture; the other 25 chapters pertain to specific aspects of architectural working drawings. Related chapters are grouped together in three divisions with colored pages to facilitate use of the book. Blue and green pages are concerned with preparation of drawings; yellow pages pertain to preparation and/or reading of drawings. When reading the book for the first time, read chapters or pages in the following order: Chapters 1, 4, 2, 3, 15, 22, Pages 126-127, 138-139; Chapters 16-21 (See applications of drafting standards and symbols in drawings shown in Chapters 23-27); Chapters 5-14; Chapters 23-27. When preparing drawings, refer to the Indices. The Drawing Index contains a list of figures and a list of examples of basic architectural working drawings; the Subject Index includes basic architectural working drawings with pages that directly relate to the drawings. To reduce drafting time and to unify working drawings, use Unifier Template 1001 illustrated in Appendix.

| 2 | GRAPHIC COMMUNICATIONS IN ARCHITECTURE | STANDARD FORMAT FOR ARCHITECTURAL WORKING DRAWINGS | |

OFFICE ARCHITECTURAL DRAFTING STANDARDS AND SYMBOLS

Uniform Office Architectural Drafting Standards and Symbols are used to produce unambiguous, unified drawings and to reduce confusion in the building industry. They do not convey information directly; consequently, they are not shown and explained in sets of architectural working drawings but are printed and issued to draftsmen. See Chapter 3.

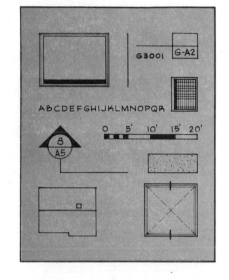

PROJECT ARCHITECTURAL DRAFTING STANDARDS AND SYMBOLS

Uniform Project Architectural Drafting Standards and Symbols are used to produce unambiguous, unified drawings and to reduce confusion in the building industry. They convey information directly and should be understandable to all members of the building industry; consequently, they are shown and explained in each set of architectural working drawings. See Chapter 15.

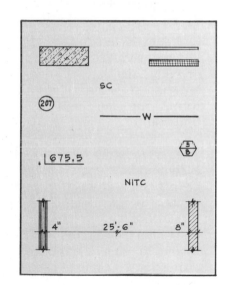

TECHNIQUES FOR PRESENTING ARCHITECTURAL DRAWINGS

Standard Techniques for Presenting Architectural Drawings are used to produce efficiently-prepared, unambiguous, unified drawings and to reduce confusion in the building industry. Like Office Architectural Drafting Standards and Symbols, Techniques for Presenting Architectural Drawings do not convey information directly; consequently, they are not shown and explained in sets of architectural working drawings but are printed and issued to draftsmen. See Chapter 22.

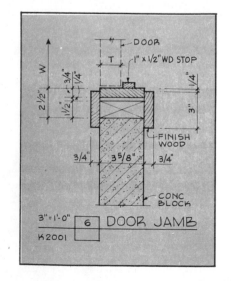

| 3 | STANDARD FORMAT FOR ARCHITECTURAL WORKING DRAWINGS | OFFICE ARCHITECTURAL DRAFTING STANDARDS AND SYMBOLS | |

OFFICE ARCHITECTURAL DRAFTING STANDARDS AND SYMBOLS

Uniform Office Architectural Drafting Standards and Symbols are used to produce unambiguous, unified drawings and to reduce confusion in the building industry. They do not convey information directly; consequently, they are not shown and explained in sets of architectural working drawings but are printed and issued to draftsmen. See illustrations and explanations of Office Architectural Drafting Standards and Symbols with directions for use in the eleven chapters listed below:

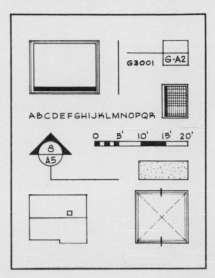

DRAWING PROCESS

See pages 126-127 for systematic incorporation of Office Architectural Drafting Standards and Symbols in drawings and pages 121-125 for drawing arrangements.

| 4 | OFFICE ARCHITECTURAL DRAFTING STANDARDS AND SYMBOLS | DRAWING TERMINOLOGY | |

DRAWING FORMS

Two drawing forms, pictorial and orthographic, are the vehicles used by design professions to convey design and construction information graphically to the building industry. Pictorial drawings are "three dimensional" drawings that convey information in a realistic manner. Pictorial drawings, used most often in architectural drawings, consist of one point perspective, two point perspective, isometric, and cavalier oblique drawings. Three point perspective, dimetric, general oblique, and cabinet oblique drawings are seldom used. Orthographic drawings are "two dimensional" drawings that convey information in an abstract or nonrealistic manner. Orthographic drawings, used most often in architectural drawings, consist of plan, elevation, and section drawings. Auxiliary view drawings are seldom required.

Pictorial Drawings are used primarily during the initial conceptual design stage of professional service to study and explain building masses, building spaces, and spatial relationships between buildings and between building components. The drawings cannot be scaled accurately in all dimensions; they normally conceal details of construction; and they require considerable time

to construct. Despite their limitations for conveying technical information, pictorial drawings are occasionally used during later stages of professional service to explain building construction. Isometric drawings are sometimes used to explain complicated construction details at corners, such as flashing installations at roof corners. Isometric and cavalier oblique drawings are normally used to explain some aspects of mechanical systems, such as drainage and vent piping.

Orthographic Drawings are used during all stages of professional service to study and explain design and construction. The drawings are diagrammatic or nonrealistic drawings that show at a reduced scale true sizes, shapes, and proportions of surfaces and sections. Surface configurations, area relationships, and internal details are effectively studied and explained with orthographic drawings. The drawings can be scaled accurately in all dimensions; they can expose details of construction; and they require little time to construct. Technical orthographic drawings are composed in part of conventions and symbols and are supplemented by notes, dimensions, and schedules.

FIGURE
1, NTS

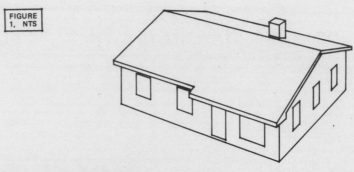

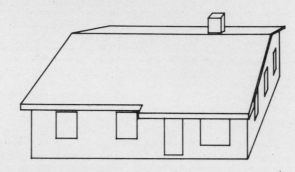

TWO POINT PERSPECTIVE

ONE POINT PERSPECTIVE

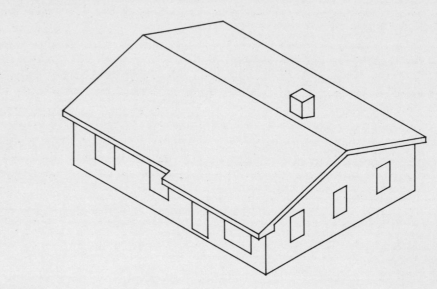

ISOMETRIC

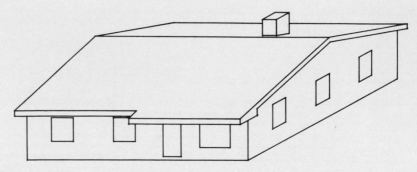

CAVALIER OBLIQUE

PICTORIAL DRAWINGS

NTS

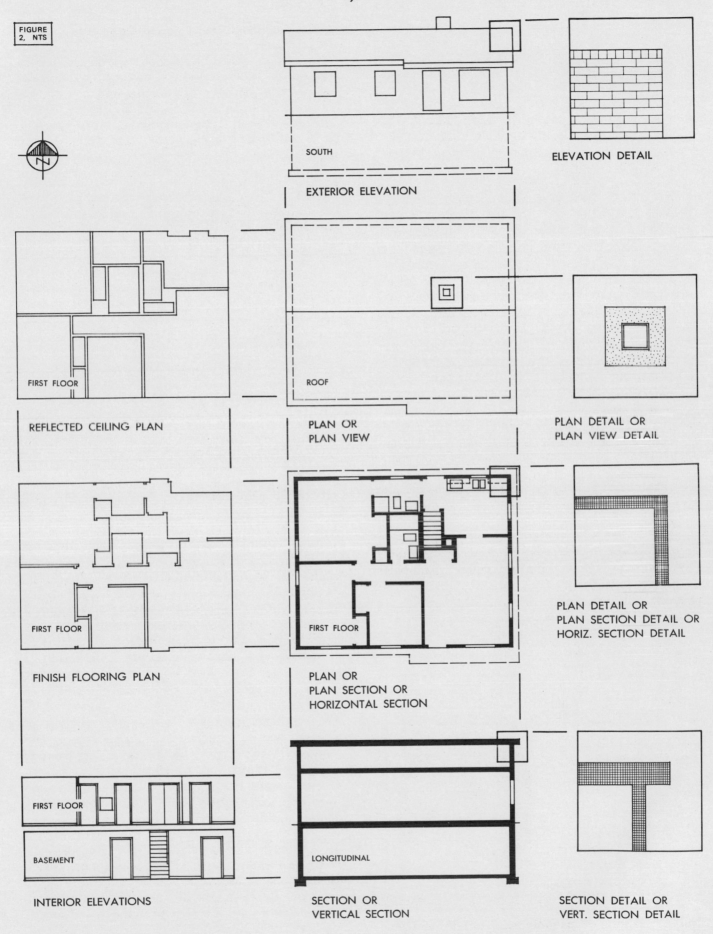

FIGURE 2, NTS

SOUTH

EXTERIOR ELEVATION

ELEVATION DETAIL

FIRST FLOOR

REFLECTED CEILING PLAN

ROOF

PLAN OR
PLAN VIEW

PLAN DETAIL OR
PLAN VIEW DETAIL

FIRST FLOOR

FINISH FLOORING PLAN

FIRST FLOOR

PLAN OR
PLAN SECTION OR
HORIZONTAL SECTION

PLAN DETAIL OR
PLAN SECTION DETAIL OR
HORIZ. SECTION DETAIL

FIRST FLOOR

BASEMENT

INTERIOR ELEVATIONS

LONGITUDINAL

SECTION OR
VERTICAL SECTION

SECTION DETAIL OR
VERT. SECTION DETAIL

ORTHOGRAPHIC DRAWINGS

NTS

DRAWING CATEGORIES

Pictorial and orthographic drawings are prepared by the design professions during distinct stages of professional service for various uses and different purposes. Drawings are grouped according to purpose into two categories: finished presentation drawings and rough study drawings that facilitate construction and preparation of finished presentation drawings.

Rough Study Drawings (also called "studies," "study drawings," or "rough sketches") are prepared in outline form showing only essential information. They are not as well-defined or noted as subsequent presentation drawings because they are prepared primarily for the design profession's own use. The drawings show design schemes or indicate solutions to construction problems. Many study drawings are usually required to formulate and analyze design and construction schemes and to arrive at problem solutions. Each scheme or solution is continually refined until criteria are satisfied or until a problem is adequately solved. If more than one scheme or solution is considered to satisfy criteria or solve a problem, each is developed to a stage where it can be individually evaluated, and then all schemes or solutions are collectively compared. The best solution is then selected and further refined, if necessary.

Rough study drawings are named in part for design professions that prepare them or for major contractors for whom information on drawings is ultimately intended. They are separated into drawing divisions.

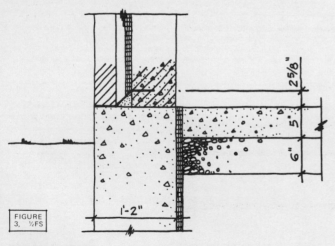

FIGURE 3, ½FS

ROUGH STUDY
ARCHITECTURAL DRAWING

Finished Presentation Drawings (usually referred to only as "drawings") are normally prepared from preceding rough study drawings to explain design and/or construction of building projects to some or all members of the building industry.

Finished presentation drawings are named in part for design professions that prepare them or for major contractors for whom information on drawings is ultimately intended (or for rough study drawings from which they are prepared), and essentially for stages of professional service during which they are drawn. They are separated into drawing divisions and drawing classifications.

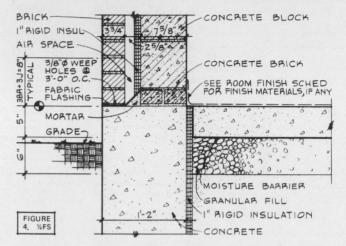

FIGURE 4, ½FS

FINISHED PRESENTATION
ARCHITECTURAL WORKING DRAWING

DRAWING DIVISIONS

Specifications supplement information shown on finished presentation drawings. They describe qualitatively what the drawings show; how materials, building components, or systems fit together or function; and where building elements can be obtained. Specifications are composed of divisions containing groups of related sections. Each section, written by or under the direction of a qualified professional, describes a basic unit of work to be performed by a particular building trade or group of construction specialists corresponding to the profession represented by the writer. Accordingly, a specification division of general work prepared by an architect and numbered and titled Division 7 - Thermal and Moisture Protection might contain sections numbered and titled Section 07300 - Shingles and Roofing Tiles, Section 07600 - Flashing and Sheet Metal, and Section 07900 - Calking and Sealants.

Rough study and finished presentation drawings, like complementary specifications, are composed of divisions. Drawings in each division, drawn by or under the direction of a qualified professional, show work to be performed by a major contractor corresponding to the profession represented by the draftsman. Accordingly, a set of drawings prepared by an electrical engineer might contain a sheet numbered and titled E2

(Electrical Sheet Number 2) - First Floor Electrical Plan and Details.

The nationally known and accepted Construction Specifications Institute's Standard Format for Construction Specifications contains the following numbered divisions:

1 - General Requirements
2 - Site Work
3 - Concrete
4 - Masonry
5 - Metals
6 - Wood and Plastics
7 - Thermal and Moisture Protection
8 - Doors and Windows
9 - Finishes
10 - Specialties
11 - Equipment
12 - Furnishings
13 - Special Construction
14 - Conveying Systems
15 - Mechanical
16 - Electrical

If some divisions are not required in a set of specifications, the numbers and titles of the divisions are nevertheless listed in the Table of Contents and voided, so that all division numbers and titles remain the same for all building projects.

Drawing Divisions relate to Specification Divisions. Based on the CSI Format for Construction Specifications, current number of recognized design profession organizations, and prevalent contracting business practices, the maximum number of distinct drawing divisions is eight. Depending on the size and complexity of a building project, this number can be reduced by combining or eliminating divisions.

Lettered Drawing Divisions are listed below, followed by possible related CSI Specification Division numbers:

A — Architectural — 1, 2, 3, 4, 5, 6, 7, 8, 9, 10, 11, 12, 13, 14.
S — Structural — 1, 2, 3, 4, 5, 6, 13, 14.
H — Heating and Ventilation — 1, 2, 10, 11, 13, 14, 15.
P — Plumbing — 1, 2, 10, 11, 13, 14, 15.
E — Electrical — 1, 2, 10, 11, 13, 14, 16.
C — Civil — 1, 2, 3, 4, 5, 6.
L — Landscaping — 1, 2, 3, 4, 5, 6.
Q — Equipment — 1, 10, 11, 12.
Z — Composite (A, S, H, P, E, C, L, Q) — 1 through 16.

DRAWING CLASSIFICATIONS

Specifications supplement information shown on finished presentation drawings. They are classified as outline or final, according to the phase of professional service in which they are prepared. Outline specifications are prepared during the schematic design and design development phases of service for use by the design professions and owner. Final specifications, usually referred to only as "specifications," are based on outline specifications. They are prepared during the construction documents phase of service for all members of the building industry.

Finished presentation drawings, like complementary specifications, are classified according to the phase of professional service in which they are prepared.

According to the American Institute of Architects' standard forms of agreement between owner and architect, the architect's basic services are divided into five distinct phases:

1. Schematic Design Phase — 15% of fee.
2. Design Development Phase — 20% of fee.
3. Construction Documents Phase — 40% of fee.
4. Bidding or Negotiation Phase — 5% of fee.
5. Construction Phase — 20% of fee.

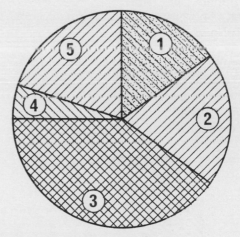

AIA standard forms of agreement between owner and architect also enumerate architect's additional services. Listed below are some additional services that require or affect drawings:

1. Making measured drawings of existing construction when required for planning additions or alterations to existing construction.
2. Revising previously approved drawings (or specifications) to accomplish changes.
3. Preparing a set of reproducible record prints of drawings showing significant changes in the work made during the construction process, based on marked-up prints, drawings, and other data furnished by the contractor to the architect.

Lettered drawing classifications based on AIA documents are listed and described below. All design profession drawings shown below are architectural drawings.

SK — Sketches are prepared during all phases of service, primarily during the schematic design phase for the purpose of explaining design concepts to the owner and/or design professions. They are usually pictorial (free-hand and/or instrument) drawings that show buildings, portions of buildings, or spaces in outline form. To keep preparation time to a minimum, sketches are invariably stylized drawings and are not as finished or complete as renderings.

R — Renderings are specialized architectural drawings normally prepared during the schematic design phase of service for the purpose of showing the owner and others how the finished building project will look from a particular viewing position. They are usually exterior view pictorial drawings, realistic in character rather than stylized. If renderings (and models) are prepared for the architect's use, the architect is responsible for preparation expenses. If renderings (and models) are prepared for the owner's use, the owner is responsible for preparation expenses and reimburses the architect.

Renderings must be of the highest quality to satisfy their purpose. To become a proficient delineator and maintain proficiency takes time, time that most architects and draftsmen cannot spare. Because of this, architects usually have renderings prepared by professional delineators. Renderings prepared by delineators are invariably of higher quality than those normally produced by architects and draftsmen, and, based on preparation time, are normally less expensive. Since architecture is the art and science of designing and constructing buildings, not the art of producing specialized pictorial drawings, it is appropriate that delineators prepare renderings.

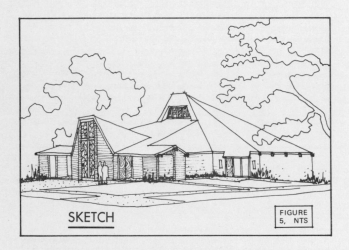

SKETCH

FIGURE 5, NTS

RENDERING BY JACK H. SWING

RENDERING

FIGURE 6, NTS

SDD – Schematic Design Drawings are prepared during the schematic design phase of service, usually from a written building program. The drawings are nontechnical drawings that show a graphic solution to the owner's and user's problems or needs. They are presented to the owner for his comments and approval. Elevations and vertical sections of buildings invariably include representations of the human figure to communicate size and scale. This vital information is communicated in plans by representations of familiar objects, such as furniture or plant material.

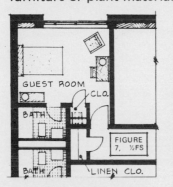

SDD FLOOR PLAN

SDD EXT ELEVATION

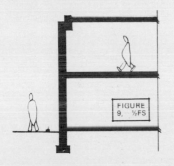

SDD SECTION

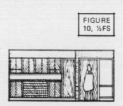

SDD INT ELEVATION

DDD – Design Development Drawings are prepared during the design development phase of service from approved schematic design drawings for the owner and design professions. The drawings are outline technical drawings that show the size and character of the entire building project in its essentials as to kinds of materials, type of structure, mechanical and electrical systems, and such other work as may be required. The purpose of the drawings is to develop and expand conceptual design. The drawings, at one time called "preliminary working drawings," are usually a necessary requirement for efficient production of working drawings.

Design development drawings for simple or small projects may be drawn carefully and developed into working drawings. For complicated or large projects they are normally drawn with less care and are used as design development drawings only.

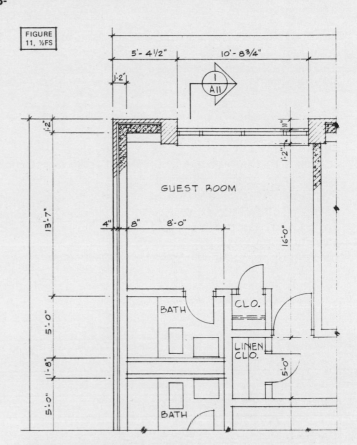

ARCH. DDD FLOOR PLAN

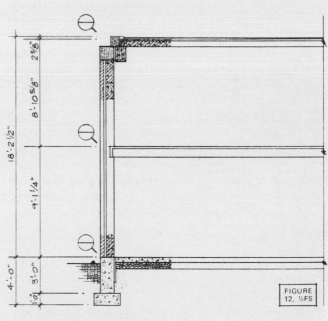

ARCH. DDD SECTION

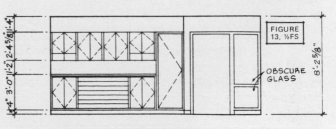

ARCH. DDD INTERIOR ELEVATION

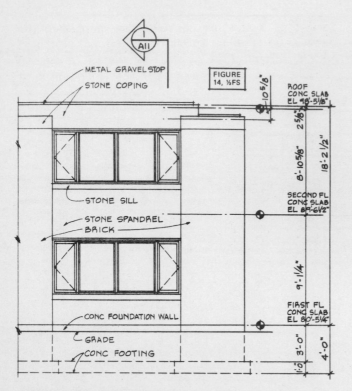

ARCH. DDD EXTERIOR ELEVATION

WD — Working Drawings are prepared during the construction documents phase of service, and sometimes during the bidding or negotiation phase of service as addenda, from approved design development drawings. They are called "working drawings" because they show graphically the work required to construct a building project. Working drawings show physical relationships between building materials, components, and systems. They are technical drawings prepared for various purposes and many people. They are used to determine contract prices, obtain building permits, secure loans and insurance, order materials, prepare shop drawings, and construct building projects. They are used by all members of the building industry, including architects, engineers, owners, estimators, contractors, building officials, lending and insurance executives, manufacturers, suppliers, fabricators, and building trades. Working drawings are a legal document between owner and contractor, and, therefore, must be understandable not only to the trained contractor but also to the owner (and other members of the building industry less familiar with working drawings).

Working drawings are composed of small scale general drawings, small scale detail drawings, large scale detail drawings, and schedules. They convey information relating to architectural, structural, heating and ventilation, plumbing, electrical, civil, landscaping, and equipment work.

The quality of each drawing in a set of working drawings should be high and constant for all building construction projects. The quantity of drawings in a set of working drawings, or thoroughness and extent of working drawings, is variable depending on many factors, including extent of professional service, amount of professional fee, type of agreement between owner and architect, type and quality of building design, type and quality of building construction, size and complexity of building project, method of selecting contractor, and type of agreement between owner and contractor.

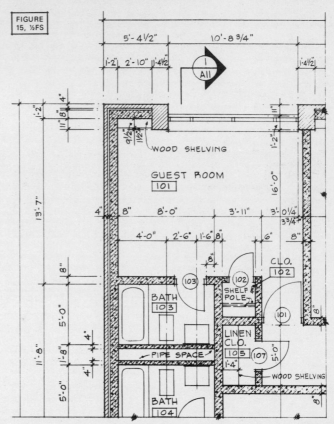

ARCH. WD FLOOR PLAN

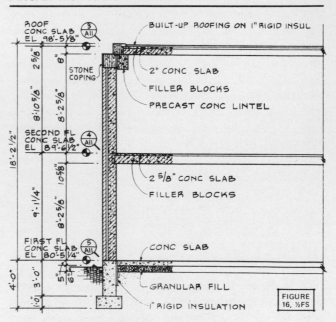

ARCH. WD SECTION

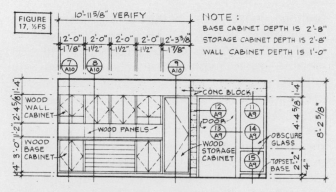

ARCH. WD INTERIOR ELEVATION

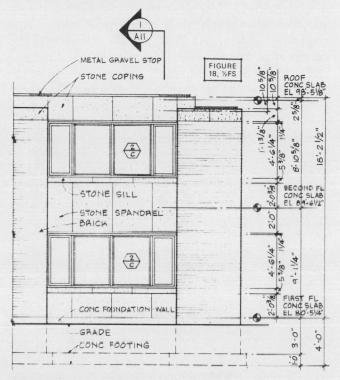

ARCH. WD EXTERIOR ELEVATION

SD — Supplemental Drawings

SD — Supplemental Drawings are prepared during the construction phase of service for all members of the building industry to serve as a guide for construction. The drawings are technical drawings prepared when necessary to correct, clarify, alter, or supplement information shown on working drawings.

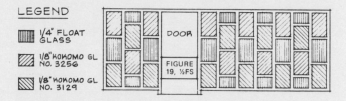

LEGEND

▦ 1/4" FLOAT GLASS

▨ 1/8" KOKOMO GL NO. 3256

▧ 1/8" KOKOMO GL NO. 3129

ARCH. SD GLASS PATTERN ELEVATION

RD — Record Drawings

RD — Record Drawings, at one time called "as-built drawings," are prepared during the construction phase of service, if directed by the owner. The drawings are usually revised working drawings that show construction changes in the work and final locations of piping, conduit, and ducts. Preparation of the drawings is a special service paid for by the owner. For an example of a working drawing and a corresponding record drawing, see Figures 20 and 21 below.

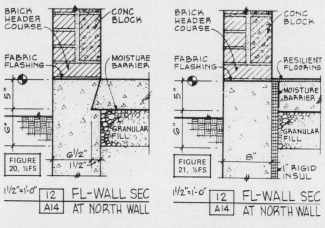

ARCH. WD   ARCH. RD

MD — Measured Drawings

MD — Measured Drawings of existing construction are required when planning additions or alterations to existing construction. The drawings are technical drawings prepared for design professions during the schematic design phase of service, prior to schematic design drawings. Rough measured drawings are sketched at the existing construction. These drawings are not to scale but are completely noted and dimensioned. Finished measured drawings are prepared in the office from them. Finished measured drawings are to scale but are not normally completely noted or dimensioned. Preparation of the drawings is a special service paid for by the owner.

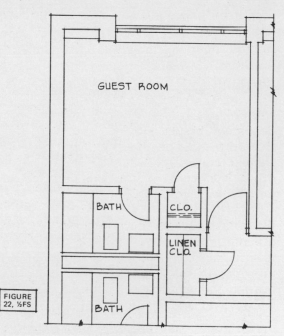

ARCH. MD FINISHED FLOOR PLAN

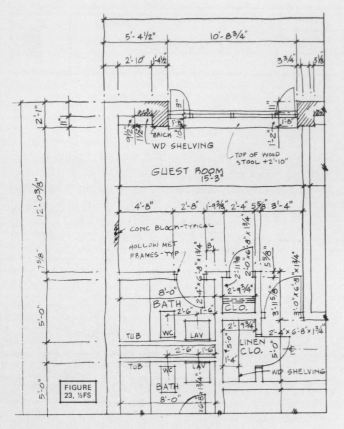

ARCH. MD ROUGH FLOOR PLAN

SHD — Shop Drawings are technical drawings prepared during the construction phase of service from working drawings, supplemental drawings, and specifications by the contracting element of the building industry. They are not prepared by the design professions. The drawings may serve as a shop and field guide for construction, fabrication, assembly, erection, or installation of particular components or elements of a building project. The design professions review and approve shop drawings (and samples) only for conformance with the design concept of the project and with the information given in the contract documents.

Shop drawings are normally required for all divisions of working drawings. Shop drawings usually required for building components shown and explained in architectural working drawings include prefabricated stairs, entrances, storefronts, windows, curtain walls, doors, millwork, cabinetwork, prefabricated partitions, prefabricated ceilings, elevators, dumbwaiters, escalators, and miscellaneous prefabricated items, such as some skylights and some tackboards.

Small scale general drawings and small scale detail drawings are normally prepared without particular consideration for shop drawings. The number of large scale detail drawings and type and amount of information contained in them are influenced by shop drawings. If shop drawings are required by the final specifications for a particular portion of the work, information shown on a large scale detail drawing involving that portion of the work is partial design and construction information concerned primarily with data required for bidding and shop drawing preparation. For example, in a window jamb large scale detail drawing showing an aluminum projected window in a plastered masonry wall, the clips that fasten the window frame to the building may be indicated graphically and noted as "clip" to explain construction; but the material, size, number, and methods of fastening the clips to the window frame and to the building are not noted. This information is included in the specifications and shown on shop drawings. All required design and construction information concerning masonry and plaster at the window jamb is shown on the architectural window jamb detail drawing, since shop drawings are not required for those portions of the work.

Design profession drawings for a particular portion of the work are not as detailed as shop drawings for that portion of the work. For large or complicated projects design profession small scale and large scale drawings are in effect reference drawings during the construction phase of service. Buildings are actually constructed following information shown on shop drawings. For comparison of information shown on a large scale detail drawing and a related shop drawing, see Figures 24 and 25 below.

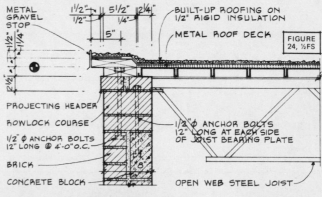

ARCH. WORKING DRAWING   ROOF-WALL SECTION

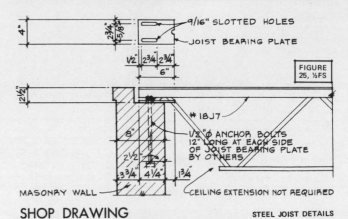

SHOP DRAWING   STEEL JOIST DETAILS

| 5 | OFFICE ARCHITECTURAL DRAFTING STANDARDS AND SYMBOLS | LINEWORK | |

GENERAL

Architectural working drawings are normally prepared on good quality transparent sheets of tracing paper, tracing cloth, or drafting film to permit tracing and/or economical reproduction; with drawing instruments to provide accuracy; and in lead to facilitate erasures. Degrees of lead vary depending on drawing sheets and "touch" of draftsman. 2H lead is often used for all linework except linework for lettering guide lines and lettering. 4H lead is often used for lettering guide lines, and HB lead is often used for lettering. H lead is sometimes used for all linework and lettering. Recommended linework standards may vary slightly if required to make drawings more understandable.

Linework by draftsmen or computers should be sharp, dense, uniform width, and constant value. Corner lines and intersecting lines should meet or overlap slightly (up to 1/32") to clearly define terminal points or enclosed areas. Four line widths: extra thick, thick, medium, and thin; and five basic line types: dotted, short dashed, long dashed, extra long dashed, and continuous are required to differentiate building components or drawing contents, allowing drawings to be more easily read and understood.

Linework should conform to standards and usages shown and explained in this chapter. For explanation of linework terminology, see Figure 26 in this chapter.

LINE WIDTHS

————————————	Extra Thick:	0.035"
————————————	Thick:	0.025"
————————————	Medium:	0.018"
————————————	Thin:	0.011"

For comparison purposes, Koh-I-Noor Rapidograph 3, 2½, 1, and 00 ink drawing points produce line widths about equal to extra thick, thick, medium, and thin line widths.

BASIC LINE TYPES

- - - - - - - - - - - - - - - - - - -	Dotted
— — — — — — — — —	Short Dashed
—— —— —— —— ——	Long Dashed
———— ———— ————	Extra Long Dashed
————————————	Continuous

NO. 1 — CONTINUOUS EXTRA THICK LINES

Use continuous extra thick lines for large-size working drawing sheet border lines, title block border lines, schedule border lines, and accent lines.

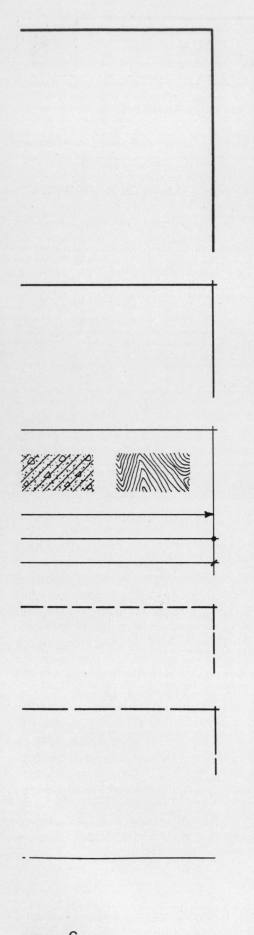

NO. 2 – CONTINUOUS THICK LINES

Use continuous thick lines for selected border lines, drawing perimeter lines, mass profile lines, and accent lines. Use continuous thick lines for detail border lines on large-size working drawing sheets; for drawing perimeter lines in some elevation and plan view drawings, in particular for floor-wall-ceiling lines in interior elevations and for wall lines in finish flooring plans and reflected ceiling plans; and for mass profile lines in large scale section details, such as finish interior and exterior wall lines in window head details. Use continuous thick lines for accent lines in the more abstract drawings to identify the most important drawing contents. For example, in structural framing plans where roof or floor decks are installed separately from framing members, show framing members in plan view by continuous thick lines.

NO. 3 – CONTINUOUS MEDIUM LINES

Use continuous medium lines for mass profile lines in small scale sections, such as finish interior and exterior wall lines in floor plans and small scale sections through buildings; for existing construction to remain; and for building component lines and building feature lines in elevation and plan view. Continuous medium lines in elevation and plan view drawings are discussed later in this chapter.

NO. 4 – CONTINUOUS THIN LINES

Use continuous thin lines for building element lines and internal mass component lines in sections, such as brick lines in large scale section details and cavity wall lines in floor plans and small scale sections through buildings; for material indications in section; for material indications in elevation; for dimension lines; and for building component lines and building feature lines in elevation and plan view. Continuous thin lines in elevation and plan view drawings are discussed later in this chapter.

NO. 5 – SHORT DASHED MEDIUM LINES

Use short dashed medium lines for hidden lines or unseen items in front of or below observer, future construction, and items not in contract. Always note dashed lines.

NO. 6 – LONG DASHED MEDIUM LINES

Use long dashed medium lines for hidden lines or unseen items in back of or above observer and for existing construction to be removed. Always note dashed lines.

NO. 7 – DOT-CONTINUOUS THIN LINES

Use dot-continuous thin lines for dimension extension lines, dimension reference lines, and projection lines.

NO. 8 – DOT-EXTRA LONG DASHED THIN LINES

Use dot-extra long dashed thin lines for center lines. Always note CL (center line) on center lines.

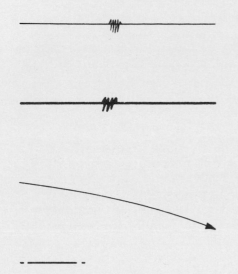

NO. 9 — CONTINUOUS THIN LINES BROKEN

Use continuous thin lines broken for break lines to limit or reduce sizes of drawings.

NO. 10 — CONTINUOUS THICK LINES BROKEN

Use continuous thick lines broken for match lines to connect separated drawings.

NO. 11 — CURVED THIN ARROW LINES WITH ARROWHEADS

Use curved thin arrow lines with arrowheads for note lines from beginning or end of notes to explained linework.

NO. 12 — DOT-DASHED-DOT MEDIUM LINES

Use dot-dashed-dot medium lines for fastening indications, such as nails, screws, and bolts, if required to clarify drawings. Always note fastening indication lines.

ELEVATION AND PLAN VIEW DRAWINGS

To make graphic information shown in elevation and plan view drawings more realistic and consequently easier to comprehend, use varying line widths to differentiate major building components, minor building components, and building features, or to give the illusion of depth.

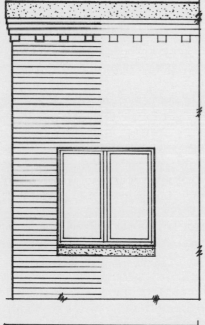

When major building components, such as exterior walls; minor building components, such as punched opening windows in exterior walls; and building features, such as corbelled brickwork below exterior wall copings are in the same general plane, use medium lines to outline major building components and thin lines to define minor building components and building features. For example, in exterior elevations, use continuous medium lines to outline masonry walls and window openings in masonry walls; and use continuous thin lines to define recessed window frames, window sashes, window mullions, bottoms and sides of window wall sills, and corbelled brickwork below exterior wall copings. Use continuous medium lines to define bottoms and sides of window wall sills and corbelled brickwork if continuous thin lines are used to indicate brickwork.

When building components are in significantly different planes, use medium lines to outline near building components and thin lines to define far building components. For example, in architectural foundation plans use continuous medium lines to outline foundation walls and continuous thin lines to define spread footings. Use varying line widths to clearly differentiate building components in plan view architectural foundation plan drawings and plan section structural framing plan drawings since material indications in elevation cannot be effectively used in these drawings.

FOUNDATION PLANS

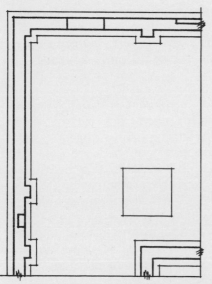

In architectural foundation plans, foundation walls and grade beams are normally shown in plan view by continuous medium lines. (In structural foundation plans, foundation walls and grade beams are normally shown in plan section by continuous medium lines with appropriate material indications in section.) Ledges, pockets, and

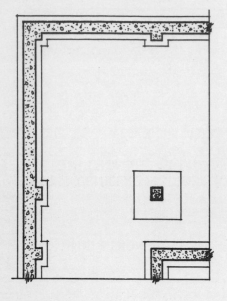

recesses at tops of foundation walls and grade beams in plan view are shown by continuous medium lines. Continuous thin lines represent wall footings, column footings, and pile caps; dashed lines represent piles. Crawl space columns in architectural foundation plans (and crawl space and basement columns in structural foundation plans) are shown in plan section by continuous thick lines with appropriate material indications in section.

In architectural foundation plans, small openings in foundation walls, such as pipe sleeve openings, are not normally indicated. Large openings in crawl space foundation walls, such as vent openings, are shown by dashed lines. Large openings in basement foundation walls, such as window openings, are not indicated on architectural foundation plans. They are indicated in plan section on architectural basement plans.

In structural foundation plans, small openings in foundation walls, such as pipe sleeve openings, are not normally indicated. Large openings in crawl space foundation walls, such as vent openings, are shown by continuous medium lines. Large openings in basement foundation walls, such as window openings, are indicated on structural foundation plans by continuous medium lines.

FRAMING PLANS

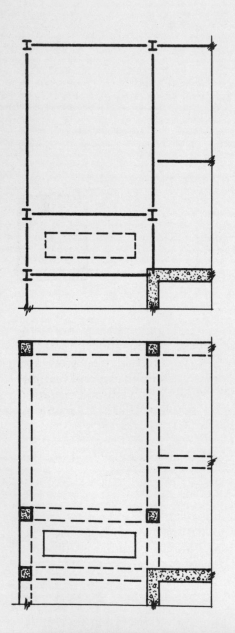

In structural framing plans that show horizontal or sloped framing members erected separately from roof or floor decks or slabs, such as steel beams supporting cast-in-place one-way solid reinforced concrete floor slabs, the framing members are normally shown for simplicity by continuous thick lines. Perimeters of decks or slabs are not normally indicated on framing plans but are indicated on detail drawings. Large openings in decks or slabs are indicated by dashed lines. Columns, piers, and bearing walls below framing members are shown by continuous thin lines. Piers and bearing walls above framing members are shown by continuous medium lines with appropriate material indications in section. Columns above framing members are shown by continuous thick lines with appropriate material indications in section. Connections of horizontal or sloped framing members to each other are indicated graphically by terminating lines representing lesser framing members about 1/16" from lines representing greater framing members. Connections of horizontal or sloped framing members to columns are indicated graphically by terminating lines representing framing members about 1/16" from lines representing columns. Miscellaneous or secondary structural members are sometimes shown on framing plans to clarify drawings. Bearing plates on piers or on bearing walls are indicated by continuous or dashed medium lines. Bridging and sag rods are indicated by dashed lines.

In structural framing plans that show horizontal or sloped framing members constructed monolithically with roof or floor slabs, such as cast-in-place reinforced concrete beams supporting one-way solid reinforced concrete floor slabs, the framing members are normally shown for clarity by double dashed lines representing widths of framing members. Perimeters of slabs and large openings in slabs are indicated by continuous medium lines. Vertical structural supports below framing members are shown by dashed lines. Piers and bearing walls above framing members are shown by continuous medium lines with appropriate material indications in section. Columns above framing members are shown by continuous thick lines with appropriate material indications in section.

LINEWORK EXPLANATION DRAWING   1½" = 1' - 0"

A door jamb plan section is shown below. Notes and dimensions on drawing are for linework explanation only.

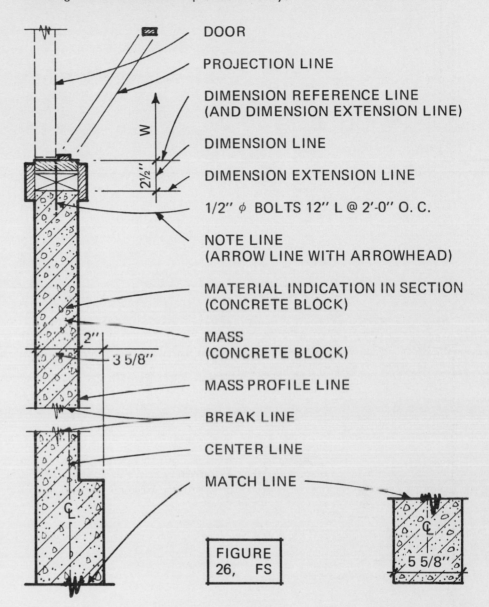

DOOR

PROJECTION LINE

DIMENSION REFERENCE LINE
(AND DIMENSION EXTENSION LINE)

DIMENSION LINE

DIMENSION EXTENSION LINE

1/2" ϕ BOLTS 12" L @ 2'-0" O. C.

NOTE LINE
(ARROW LINE WITH ARROWHEAD)

MATERIAL INDICATION IN SECTION
(CONCRETE BLOCK)

MASS
(CONCRETE BLOCK)

MASS PROFILE LINE

BREAK LINE

CENTER LINE

MATCH LINE

FIGURE
26,   FS

Linework in plan section and vertical section drawings normally consists of medium and thin lines or thick, medium, and thin lines. A greater variety of line widths is often required in plan view and elevation drawings to differentiate building components and features or to give the illusion of depth. Linework in plan view and elevation drawings often consists of thick, thick-medium (0.021"), medium, medium-thin (0.014"), and thin lines.

| 6 | **OFFICE ARCHITECTURAL DRAFTING STANDARDS AND SYMBOLS** | **LETTERING** | |

GENERAL

Lettering, or printing, or typewriting in architectural working drawings should consist of vertical capital letters that are judiciously sized and spaced permitting notes, dimensions, and titles on drawings to be easily read. Lettering should have a minimum thickness of 0.018" (medium line width). Lead is normally used for lettering to facilitate erasures. Degrees of lead vary depending on drawing sheets and "touch" of draftsman. 4H lead is often used for lettering guidelines, and HB lead is often used for lettering. H lead is sometimes used for lettering guidelines and lettering. Recommended lettering widths and horizontal spacings for letters may be reduced slightly if required to fit notes, dimensions, and titles on drawings in confined areas. Wider spacings may be used for letters in titles so that titles can extend to full widths of drawings above.

LETTERING HEIGHTS AND VERTICAL SPACINGS

Like linework, lettering should be sharp, dense, uniform width, and constant value. Lettering should conform to lettering heights and vertical spacings shown on this page. Use vertical oblong letters that are slightly higher than they are wide or block letters that are about as wide as they are high, except for I, J, M, and W. I and J are not as wide as they are high, and M and W are wider than they are high. Use light, thin guidelines for lettering to control letter heights. The guidelines should not show on copies of drawings.

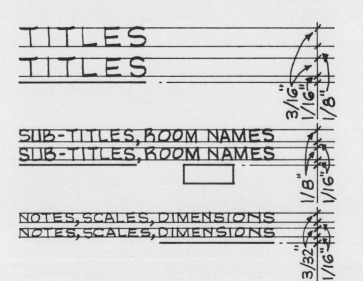

LETTERING STYLES

Lettering styles, like handwriting, vary for each draftsman. Examples of clear lettering styles (not lettering heights and vertical spacings), taken from different comic strips in Sunday and weekday newspapers, are shown on the following page. The examples also show proper horizontal spacings for letters (1/32" minimum) and acceptable range of thicknesses for letters.

ABCDEFGHIJKLM
NOPQRSTUVWXYZ
0123456789 - 1/2

ABCDEFGHIJKLM
NOPQRSTUVWXYZ
0123456789 - 1/2

ABCDEFGHIJKLMNOPQRSTU
VWXYZ   0123456789 - 1/2

ABCDEFGHIJKLMNOPQRSTUVWXYZ
0123456789-1/2   TYPEWRITER

ABCDEFGHIJKLMNOPQRSTUVWXYZ
0123456789-½   VARITYPER

I CAN GET A NEW HOUSE?

I'VE DECIDED TO CALL OFF MY STRIKE.

SO I'M GOING TO REDUCE YOUR SENTENCE TO ONLY THIRTY DAYS!

HOW MANY GRAINS OF SAND DO YOU THINK THERE ARE ON THE BEACH?

YOU WOULD, TOO, IF YOU WERE AS OLD AS THAT SUIT!

THANK YOU SO MUCH FOR EVERYTHING!

OPERATOR, CAN'T YOU GET THROUGH TO MY PARTY IN NEW YORK?

SHE'S THREATENING TO FILE A GRIEVANCE

HAVE YOU EVER CONSIDERED SEEING A PSYCHIATRIST?

YES, MADAM-- I AM HE!

WE HAD A BREAKDOWN IN COMMUNICATIONS!

IT'S OBVIOUS HE'S NEVER BEEN TO A DOG FIGHT

... AND THE CHARTER COMPANY CALLED TO SAY THAT THE OWNER OF THE LOAD WILL BE RIDING ALONG...

IT IS TIME FER YER BATH!!

THIS IS A PERFECT PLACE FOR US!

NO, DOES IT FLY AROUND LOOSE?

WHAT ARE ALL THOSE PEOPLE DOING IN YOUR GARAGE?

I THOUGHT YOU WAS HUNGRY!

THE WIND, I GUESS! I'M TAKING IT TO THE BASEMENT TO FIX...

HAVE A GOOD TIME

DID YOU GET HIS LICENSE NUMBER?

YOU CAN, IF YOU THINK YOU CAN!

DO YOU KNOW HIS ROOM NUMBER?

THAT'S RIGHT! NO MATTER HOW SEPARATED WE ARE BY DISTANCE, WE CAN BE BOUND TOGETHER BY PRAYER!

THANKS FOR COMING, DIRECTOR.

OF COURSE!

DOLLARS TO DOUGHNUTS SHE'LL NEVER HAVE TO PUSH IT!

HERE'S A HOUSE THAT SOUNDS GOOD--- IT HAS THREE BATHROOMS

I FEEL LIKE I WALKED IN IN THE MIDDLE OF THE PICTURE

THIS PROMISES TO DEVELOP INTO ONE OF THOSE BLOOD FEUDS BETWEEN TWO GREAT FAMILIES. ONE THAT MIGHT LAST A HUNDRED YEARS. THE QUEEN HAS THEM BROUGHT BEFORE HER.

| 7 | OFFICE ARCHITECTURAL DRAFTING STANDARDS AND SYMBOLS | MATERIAL INDICATIONS IN ELEVATION | |

GENERAL

Identify by notes materials in elevation drawings, such as finish wall surfaces; and materials in plan view drawings, such as finish flooring, finish ceiling, and finish roofing surfaces. If notes alone are inadequate to clearly identify materials, or if drawings are difficult to understand, identify materials in elevation and plan view drawings by notes and material indications in elevation shown in this chapter. The indications will differentiate drawing contents and make drawings pictorial in character.

For simplicity and drafting economy, material indications in elevation linework is limited to dots, straight and curved nonintersecting short dashed lines, and straight and curved nonintersecting continuous lines. The linework limitation necessitates similar material indications in elevation for some materials. Where materials with similar material indications meet or overlap in elevation or plan view drawings, alter the indications slightly to clearly differentiate surfaces.

In vertical section drawings do not identify materials in vertical surfaces beyond section plane unless identifications are required to explain sections, or unless vertical surfaces serve as exterior elevations or interior elevations. In plan section drawings do not identify materials in horizontal surfaces beyond section plane unless identifications are required to explain sections, or unless horizontal surfaces serve as finish flooring plans or roof plans. Do not indicate floor materials graphically or identify them by notes on small scale floor plans. Floor materials are identified in room finish schedules; if necessary, they are indicated by notes and material indications in elevation on finish flooring plans.

Material indications in elevation may vary slightly on drawings to suit different drawing scales or sizes or to accommodate different drafting techniques. If required, formulate additional material indications in elevation to complement material indications in elevation shown in this chapter using dots, straight and curved nonintersecting short dashed lines, and straight and curved nonintersecting continuous lines.

MATERIAL INDICATIONS IN ELEVATION

Note No. 1. Horizontal joint lines and notes comprise material indication in elevation.
Note No. 2. Horizontal and vertical joint lines and notes comprise material indication in elevation.

ACOUSTIC TILE	BRICK (see note no. 1)	CERAMIC TILE (see note no. 2)	CLAY TILE (see note no. 1)	CONCRETE: CAST-IN-PLACE
CONCRETE: PRECAST	CONCRETE: BLOCK (see note no. 1)	CONCRETE: BRICK (see note no. 1)	GLASS BLOCK (see note no. 2)	GRANITE
MARBLE	MATERIAL: AS NOTED ON DRAWINGS	METAL	PLASTER	PLASTER BOARD- GYPSUM BOARD- DRYWALL

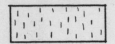

SLATE

STONE:
CUT

see note
no. 2

STONE:
RUBBLE

see note
no. 2

STRUCTURAL
CLAY FACING
TILE

WOOD

| 8 | OFFICE ARCHITECTURAL DRAFTING STANDARDS AND SYMBOLS | ARCHITECTURAL CONVENTIONS | |

GENERAL

Architectural conventions are essentially "shorthand" notations of movable building components and their operations in small scale drawings, particularly in small scale section drawings. They show primarily windows and doors and their operations in walls and interior partitions.

WINDOWS

Windows are weathertight rigid units or assemblies installed in exterior wall openings to provide any or all of the following: vision, natural light, and natural ventilation. Windows consist of framed glass panels; frames without mullions that contain one or more sashes; or frames with mullions that contain a minimum of two sashes, two fixed panels (that are usually glass), or one sash and one fixed panel. Window operating sashes slide vertically or horizontally, or project, swing, or pivot in or out to provide natural ventilation or to permit cleaning of both interior and exterior glass surfaces from inside of buildings.

Windows are typed according to sash operations. Common window types include framed glass panel, fixed sash, double hung, single hung, horizontal sliding (or horizontal rolling), projected, casement, reversible (or pivoted), awning, jalousie (or louver), and combination windows. Window types are identified in working drawings by sash operating indications in windows on exterior elevations or by sash operating indications in isolated exterior elevations of windows. Sash operating indications consist of notes and symbols in operating sashes.

Windows installed on the site in prepared punched wall openings are called "punched opening windows." They are explained in isolated exterior elevations of window types and window detail drawings. Windows installed at the factory in prefabricated walls (usually curtain walls) are considered integral parts of wall units. They are explained in exterior elevations and wall detail drawings.

Window indications in exterior and interior elevations, including window sashes, frames, mullions, trim, heads, jambs, sills, exterior wall sills, and interior wall stools are drawn accurately to represent proposed windows and window installations. Window frames only are normally shown in small scale section drawings; window sash and glass are seldom indicated. Small window sash and frame thicknesses and intricate frame section profiles prevent accurate representations of window types and window installations in small scale section drawings. Information contained in window types, window details, and specifications make accurate representations unnecessary. Window hardware is not normally shown in window elevations, plans, or details.

If required to convey necessary design and construction information, window indications in small scale section drawings are unique indications that are simplified versions of window details. If unique window indications are not required, stylized or conventionalized indications are used. These indications are suitable for buildings designed to incorporate conventional materials and methods of construction. In stylized indications, projecting sills and stools are normally shown flush on plans and sections for drafting convenience. If projection indications are required to clearly explain design and construction, they are shown on stylized window indications.

STYLIZED WINDOW INDICATIONS IN SECTIONS NTS

Notes and dimensions indicated in vertical sections shown below are for explanatory purposes only; they are not indicated in small scale drawings.

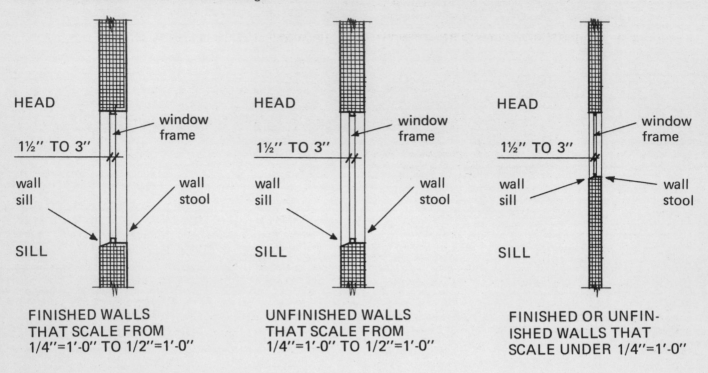

FINISHED WALLS
THAT SCALE FROM
1/4''=1'-0'' TO 1/2''=1'-0''

UNFINISHED WALLS
THAT SCALE FROM
1/4''=1'-0'' TO 1/2''=1'-0''

FINISHED OR UNFIN-
ISHED WALLS THAT
SCALE UNDER 1/4''=1'-0''

STYLIZED WINDOW INDICATIONS IN PLANS NTS

Notes and dimensions indicated in plan sections shown below are for explanatory purposes only; they are not indicated in small scale drawings.

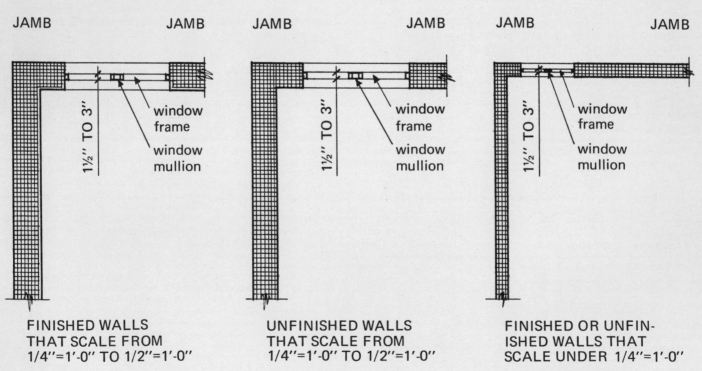

FINISHED WALLS
THAT SCALE FROM
1/4''=1'-0'' TO 1/2''=1'-0''

UNFINISHED WALLS
THAT SCALE FROM
1/4''=1'-0'' TO 1/2''=1'-0''

FINISHED OR UNFIN-
ISHED WALLS THAT
SCALE UNDER 1/4''=1'-0''

WINDOW INDICATIONS IN ELEVATION NTS

Sash operations are indicated by notes and symbols in sashes. Notes outside of window elevations shown below are for explanatory purposes only; they are not indicated in drawings. Wall sills and window trim at heads and jambs are not shown on isolated exterior elevations of windows. For illustrative purposes four combination windows are shown below.

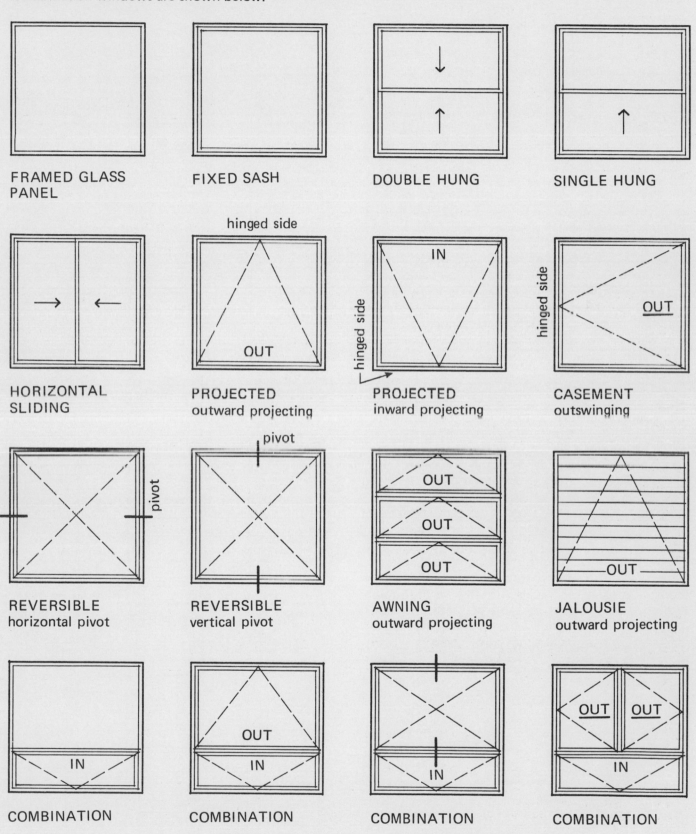

FRAMED GLASS PANEL

FIXED SASH

DOUBLE HUNG

SINGLE HUNG

HORIZONTAL SLIDING

PROJECTED
outward projecting

PROJECTED
inward projecting

CASEMENT
outswinging

REVERSIBLE
horizontal pivot

REVERSIBLE
vertical pivot

AWNING
outward projecting

JALOUSIE
outward projecting

COMBINATION

COMBINATION

COMBINATION

COMBINATION

DOORS

Doors are movable units or assemblies that close openings in walls or partitions to which they are attached. Doors swing, slide vertically or horizontally, pivot, revolve, fold sideways, or roll down to close door openings. Depending on door functions and operations, doors are rigid or flexible, one piece or sectional. Door openings or doorways are usually specially framed and cased to accommodate doors.

Doors are typed according to general door construction; namely, rigid, flexible, one piece, or sectional; appearance or style, such as flush, flush glazed, or panel; and door closing and opening operations. Common door types include hinged (or swinging), pivot, balanced, sliding (horizontal), bi-fold, folding (or accordian), rolling (vertical), overhead (sectional), vertical lift (one piece), and revolving doors. Door types are identified in working drawings by isolated door elevations and by door operating indications in doorways on plans. Door indications comprise part or all of door operating indications, and are normally shown as single lines. If door thicknesses significantly affect design or construction, such as vault doors, door indications are drawn showing door plan section profile.

Door indications in exterior and interior elevations, including doors, door frames, trim, heads, jambs, and sills are drawn accurately to represent proposed doors and door frame installations. Doors are normally indicated by single lines on small scale plans and by continuous or dashed lines in detail drawings. They are not normally indicated in small scale vertical section drawings. Small door frame thicknesses and intricate frame section profiles prevent accurate representation of door frame installations in small scale section drawings. Information contained in door indications in elevations (elevations of door types), door and door operating indications in plan, door frame details, and specifications make accurate representations unnecessary. Door hardware is not normally shown in door elevations, plans, or details.

If required to convey necessary design and construction information, door frame indications in small scale section drawings are unique indications that are simplified versions of door frame details. Vault and walk-in refrigerator doors are examples of doors that require unique door frame (and door) indications. If unique door frame indications are not required, stylized or conventionalized indications are used. These indications are suitable for buildings designed to incorporate conventional materials and methods of construction.

COMMON DOOR STYLES NTS

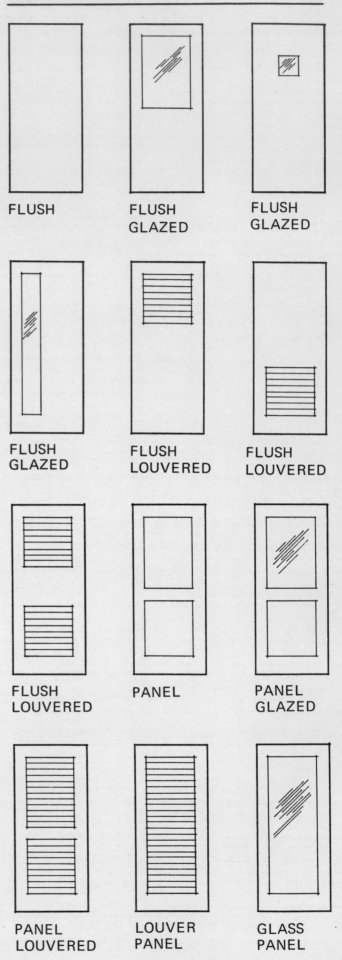

FLUSH

FLUSH GLAZED

FLUSH GLAZED

FLUSH GLAZED

FLUSH LOUVERED

FLUSH LOUVERED

FLUSH LOUVERED

PANEL

PANEL GLAZED

PANEL LOUVERED

LOUVER PANEL

GLASS PANEL

DOOR AND DOOR OPERATING INDICATIONS IN PLAN   NTS

Doorway plan sections shown below indicate walls finished one side and unfinished one side.

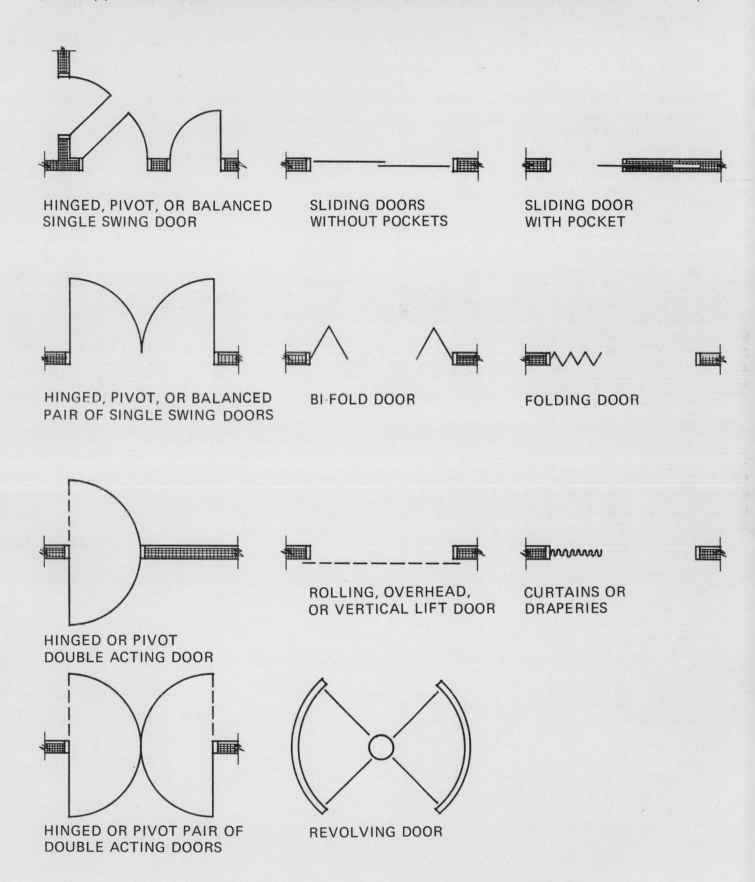

HINGED, PIVOT, OR BALANCED
SINGLE SWING DOOR

SLIDING DOORS
WITHOUT POCKETS

SLIDING DOOR
WITH POCKET

HINGED, PIVOT, OR BALANCED
PAIR OF SINGLE SWING DOORS

BI-FOLD DOOR

FOLDING DOOR

HINGED OR PIVOT
DOUBLE ACTING DOOR

ROLLING, OVERHEAD,
OR VERTICAL LIFT DOOR

CURTAINS OR
DRAPERIES

HINGED OR PIVOT PAIR OF
DOUBLE ACTING DOORS

REVOLVING DOOR

STYLIZED DOOR FRAME INDICATIONS IN SECTIONS   NTS

Notes and dimensions indicated in sections shown below are for explanatory purposes only; they are not indicated in small scale drawings.

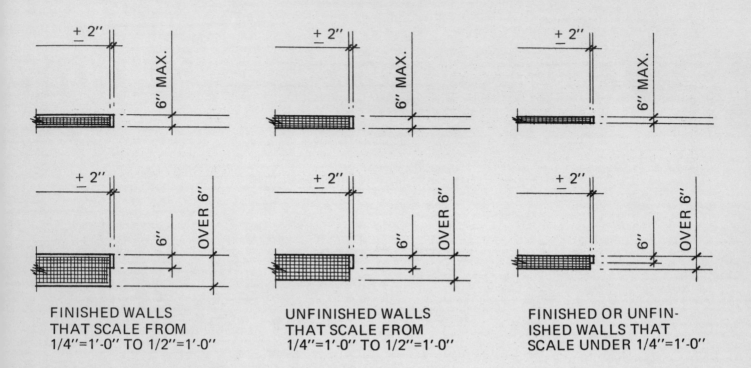

FINISHED WALLS
THAT SCALE FROM
1/4"=1'-0" TO 1/2"=1'-0"

UNFINISHED WALLS
THAT SCALE FROM
1/4"=1'-0" TO 1/2"=1'-0"

FINISHED OR UNFIN-
ISHED WALLS THAT
SCALE UNDER 1/4"=1'-0"

PLAN SECTIONS OF COMMON INTERIOR PARTITIONS   NTS

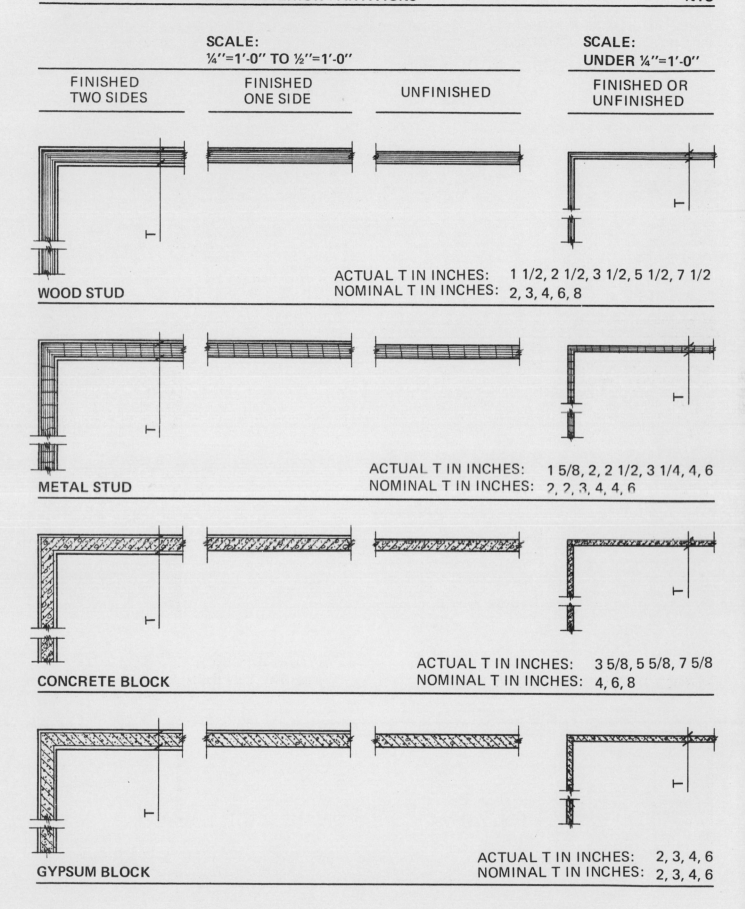

SCALE:
¼''=1'-0'' TO ½''=1'-0''

SCALE:
UNDER ¼''=1'-0''

| FINISHED TWO SIDES | FINISHED ONE SIDE | UNFINISHED | FINISHED OR UNFINISHED |

WOOD STUD

ACTUAL T IN INCHES: 1 1/2, 2 1/2, 3 1/2, 5 1/2, 7 1/2
NOMINAL T IN INCHES: 2, 3, 4, 6, 8

METAL STUD

ACTUAL T IN INCHES: 1 5/8, 2, 2 1/2, 3 1/4, 4, 6
NOMINAL T IN INCHES: 2, 2, 3, 4, 4, 6

CONCRETE BLOCK

ACTUAL T IN INCHES: 3 5/8, 5 5/8, 7 5/8
NOMINAL T IN INCHES: 4, 6, 8

GYPSUM BLOCK

ACTUAL T IN INCHES: 2, 3, 4, 6
NOMINAL T IN INCHES: 2, 3, 4, 6

NOTE:
FINISH PARTITION LINES ARE NORMALLY DRAWN 1/32'' FROM ROUGH PARTITION LINES.

PLAN SECTIONS OF COMMON INTERIOR PARTITIONS   NTS

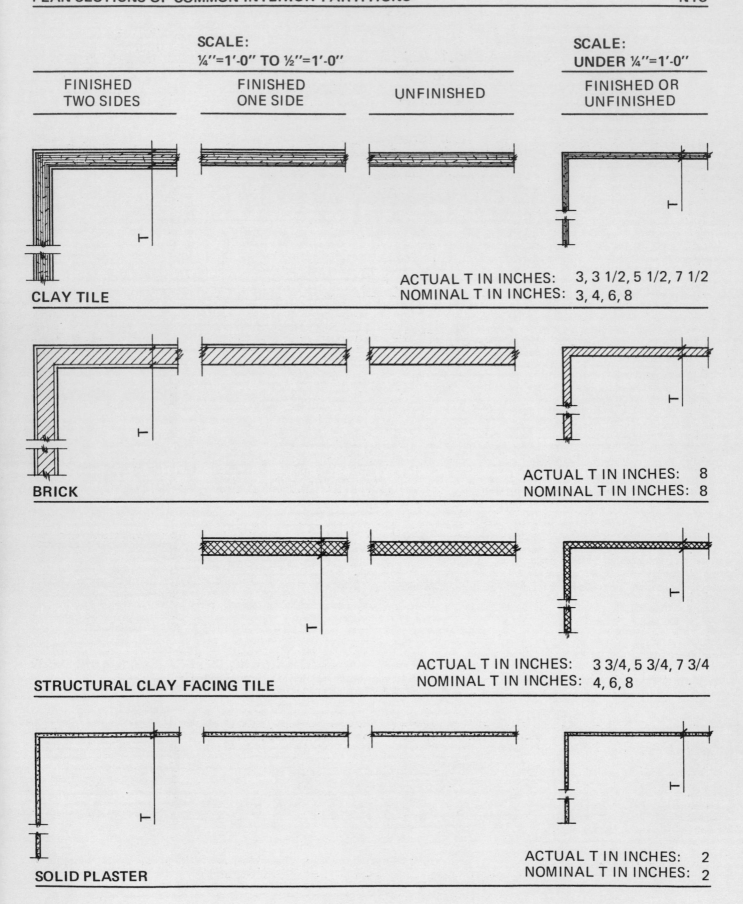

SCALE:
¼"=1'-0" TO ½"=1'-0"

SCALE:
UNDER ¼"=1'-0"

FINISHED TWO SIDES | FINISHED ONE SIDE | UNFINISHED | FINISHED OR UNFINISHED

CLAY TILE

ACTUAL T IN INCHES: 3, 3 1/2, 5 1/2, 7 1/2
NOMINAL T IN INCHES: 3, 4, 6, 8

BRICK

ACTUAL T IN INCHES: 8
NOMINAL T IN INCHES: 8

STRUCTURAL CLAY FACING TILE

ACTUAL T IN INCHES: 3 3/4, 5 3/4, 7 3/4
NOMINAL T IN INCHES: 4, 6, 8

SOLID PLASTER

ACTUAL T IN INCHES: 2
NOMINAL T IN INCHES: 2

NOTE:
FINISH PARTITION LINES ARE NORMALLY DRAWN 1/32" FROM ROUGH PARTITION LINES.

PLAN SECTIONS OF COMMON EXTERIOR WALLS   **NTS**

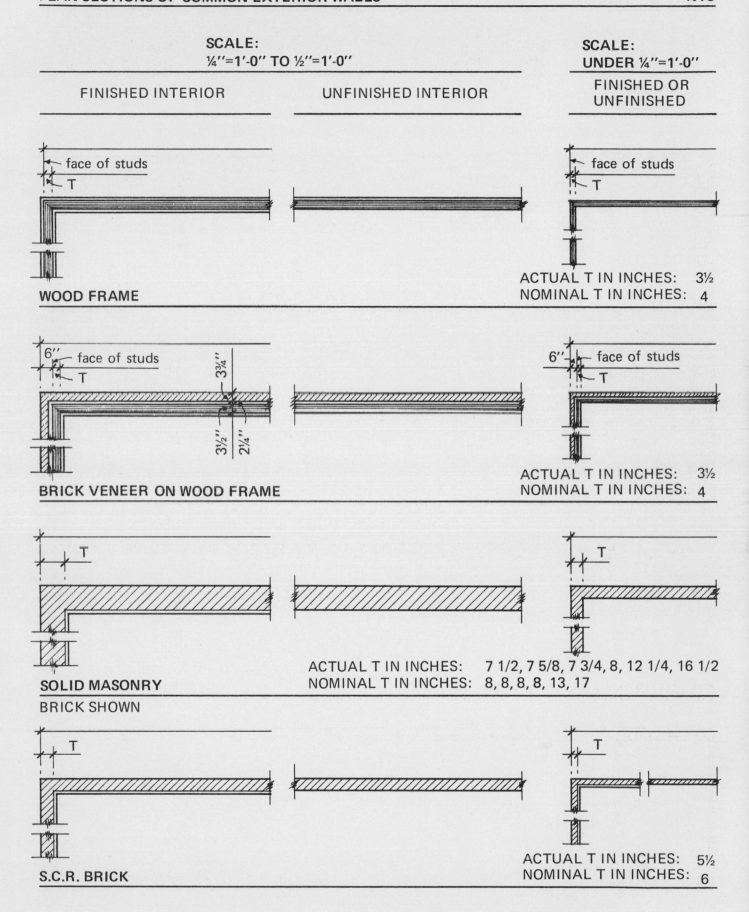

SCALE:
¼″=1′-0″ TO ½″=1′-0″

SCALE:
UNDER ¼″=1′-0″

FINISHED INTERIOR   UNFINISHED INTERIOR   FINISHED OR UNFINISHED

face of studs
T

WOOD FRAME

ACTUAL T IN INCHES: 3½
NOMINAL T IN INCHES: 4

6″ face of studs
T

3¾″
3½″
2¼″

6″ face of studs
T

BRICK VENEER ON WOOD FRAME

ACTUAL T IN INCHES: 3½
NOMINAL T IN INCHES: 4

T

T

SOLID MASONRY
BRICK SHOWN

ACTUAL T IN INCHES: 7 1/2, 7 5/8, 7 3/4, 8, 12 1/4, 16 1/2
NOMINAL T IN INCHES: 8, 8, 8, 8, 13, 17

T

T

S.C.R. BRICK

ACTUAL T IN INCHES: 5½
NOMINAL T IN INCHES: 6

NOTE:
FINISH WALL LINES ARE NORMALLY DRAWN 1/32″ FROM ROUGH WALL LINES.

PLAN SECTIONS OF COMMON EXTERIOR WALLS   **NTS**

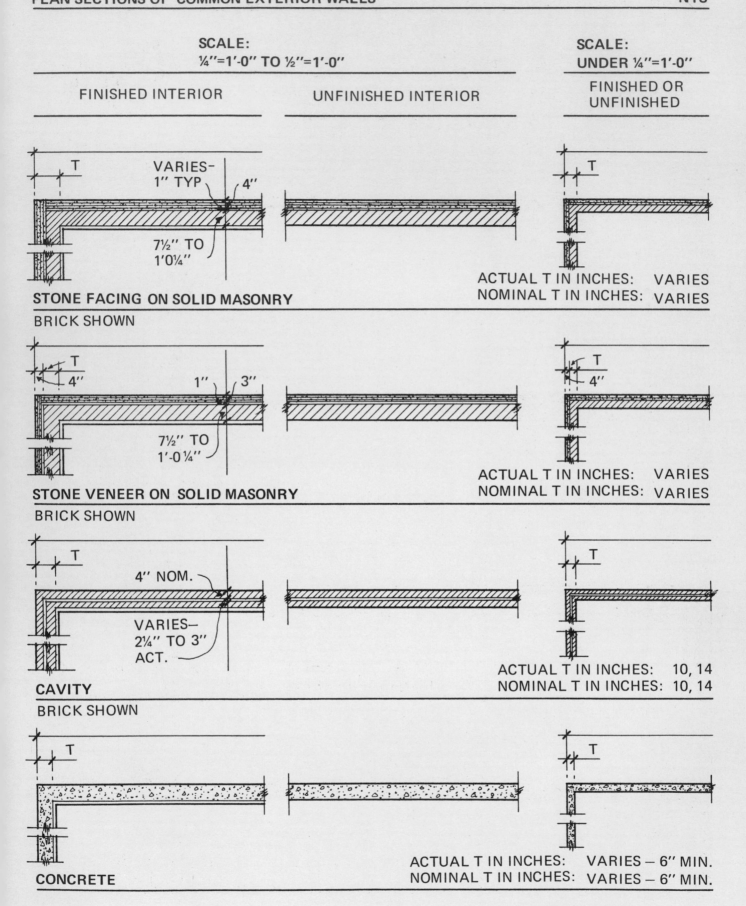

SCALE:
¼"=1'-0" TO ½"=1'-0"

SCALE:
UNDER ¼"=1'-0"

FINISHED INTERIOR | UNFINISHED INTERIOR | FINISHED OR UNFINISHED

T

VARIES-
1" TYP   4"

7½" TO
1'0¼"

ACTUAL T IN INCHES: VARIES
NOMINAL T IN INCHES: VARIES

STONE FACING ON SOLID MASONRY
BRICK SHOWN

T
4"

1"   3"

7½" TO
1'-0¼"

ACTUAL T IN INCHES: VARIES
NOMINAL T IN INCHES: VARIES

STONE VENEER ON SOLID MASONRY
BRICK SHOWN

T

4" NOM.

VARIES—
2¼" TO 3"
ACT.

ACTUAL T IN INCHES: 10, 14
NOMINAL T IN INCHES: 10, 14

CAVITY
BRICK SHOWN

T

ACTUAL T IN INCHES: VARIES — 6" MIN.
NOMINAL T IN INCHES: VARIES — 6" MIN.

CONCRETE

NOTE:
FINISH WALL LINES ARE NORMALLY DRAWN 1/32" FROM ROUGH WALL LINES.

COLUMN REFERENCE LINE INDICATIONS

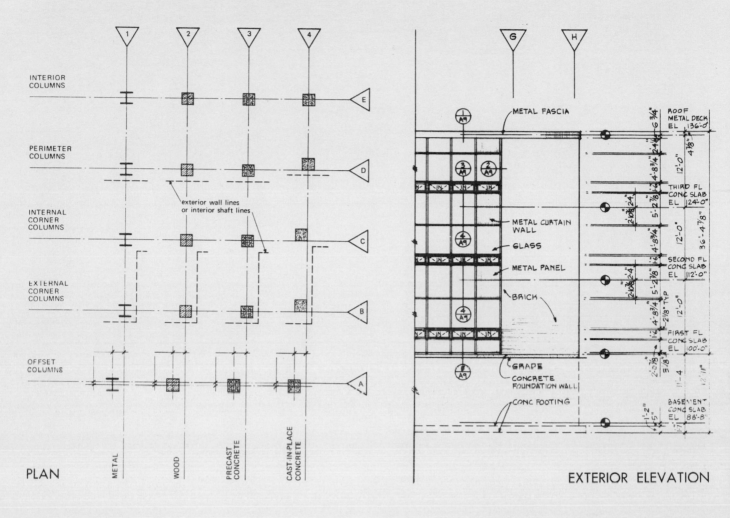

PLAN

EXTERIOR ELEVATION

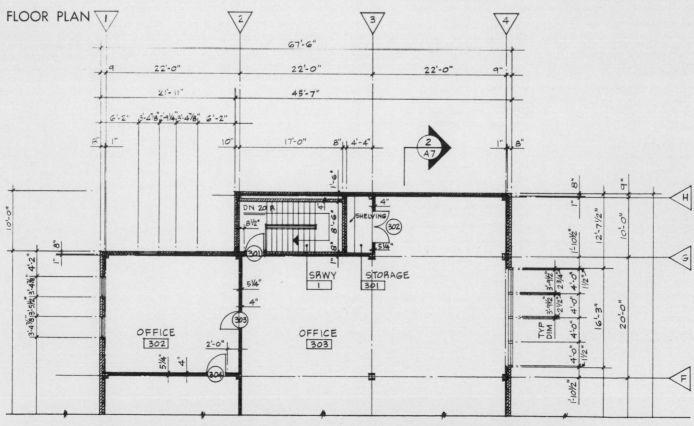

FLOOR PLAN

| 9 | OFFICE ARCHITECTURAL DRAFTING STANDARDS AND SYMBOLS | SECTION INDICATION SYMBOLS | |

GENERAL

Section Indication Symbols, shown most often on small scale general drawings, are used to identify general or exact locations of sections and details in buildings and to reference drawings. They are composed of the Drawing Reference Symbol (shown and explained in Chapter 18) modified. Section Indication Symbols shown below are drawn to scale. Place them on drawings as directed below.

KEY PLAN SECTION SYMBOL

Show the Key Plan Section Symbol on key plans for wall sections and/or small scale sections through buildings in lieu of Major Section Symbols on small scale plans.

SECTION CUT SYMBOL

Show the Section Cut Symbol on plans and elevations for section details not referenced by Minor Section Symbols, Major Section Symbols, Door Reference Symbols, or Window Reference Symbols. If necessary to show direction of section view, place a point line on the symbol similar to point line on Section Point Symbol.

SECTION POINT SYMBOL

Show the Section Point Symbol primarily on small scale horizontal and vertical sections and particularly on small scale (vertical) sections through buildings and stair sections, near areas detailed. Indicate the general area detailed by a thick (point) line on the symbol pointing to the area detailed.

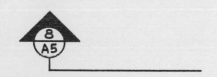

MINOR SECTION SYMBOL

Show the Minor Section Symbol on plans and elevations for small scale partial (vertical) sections through buildings and other significant building sections other than wall sections and/or small scale complete (vertical) sections through buildings.

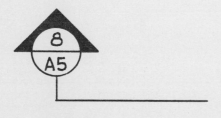

MAJOR SECTION SYMBOL

Show the Major Section Symbol on small scale plans and exterior elevations for wall sections and/or small scale complete (vertical) sections through buildings. Indicate cutting plane offsets on small scale plans by thick lines. Do not show the Major Section Symbol on exterior elevations for small scale plan sections through buildings.

ROOM ELEVATION SYMBOL

Show the Room Elevation Symbol on detail floor plans for complicated rooms only. Room Finish Schedules normally indicate locations of room elevations in a set of architectural working drawings (in Detail Sheet column).

TITLE REFERENCE SYMBOL (REFERENCE SYMBOL)

Section Indication Symbols and the Title Reference Symbol (shown and explained in Chapter 18) are interrelated. The contents of both symbols; namely, drawing number and sheet number on which drawing is presented are the same.

NOTE:

In Section Indication Symbols and Title Reference Symbol shown in this chapter, 8 is drawing number (on sheet A5), and A5 is sheet number on which drawing is presented (architectural sheet number 5). If necessary, sizes of Section Indication Symbols shown above may be made slightly larger on drawings to accommodate lettering in symbols or slightly larger or smaller on drawings to suit scales of drawings. Locations for Section Indication Symbols in a set of architectural working drawings given in this chapter are general locations. For specific locations, see Schedule of Locations for Drafting Standards and Symbols in Chapter 25.

| 10 | OFFICE ARCHITECTURAL DRAFTING STANDARDS AND SYMBOLS | ARCHITECTURAL WORK- ING DRAWING SECTIONS | |

GENERAL

Exact contents of a set of architectural working drawings vary for each building construction project, but general contents, contained in small scale general drawings, small scale detail drawings, large scale detail drawings, and schedules are similar.

Arrange drawings in sets of architectural working drawings in order of building construction with small scale general drawings first followed by detail drawings and schedules. Derive sheet titles from sheet contents. Use simple consecutive numbers (D1, D2, D3, etc.) for sheet numbers on all small-size detail sheets. On large-size working drawing sheets, use simple consecutive numbers (A1, A2, A3, etc.) for sheet numbers on all projects if possible, and compound consecutive numbers (A-A1, B-A1, B-A2, B-A3, C-A1, C-A2, etc.) for sheet numbers on large or complicated projects if necessary.

For small or medium projects, sheet contents and number of sheets can be accurately determined during the initial sheet layout stage of working drawing preparation, permitting large-size working drawing sheets to be titled and numbered consecutively (A1, A2, A3, etc.) before actual preparation of working drawings begins. Efficient preparation of working drawings requires that sheets be numbered as soon as practical to permit immediate and continuous referencing of detail drawings during the drawing stage of working drawing preparation. For some large or complicated projects, sheet contents and number of sheets may be difficult if not impossible to accurately determine during the initial sheet layout stage. When it is impossible to accurately estimate the number of working drawing sheets, use a flexible sheet numbering system that permits sheet numbers for large-size working drawing sheets to be assigned before and during the drawing stage (L-A1, L-A2, L-A3).

ARCHITECTURAL WORKING DRAWING SECTIONS

To facilitate numbering of large-size working drawing sheets for some large or complicated projects, to facilitate cataloging of selected detail drawings, and to provide a checklist for sheet layouts (explained in Chapter 26), architectural working drawings are divided into lettered sections composed of similar or related drawing content. If necessary, use compound consecutive numbers for sheet numbers, composed of section letters (A, B, C, etc.) and consecutive sheet numbers in sections (A1, A2, A3, etc.). For example, sheet number L-A3 would be the third sheet in section L (Interior Elevations). Architectural Working Drawing lettered sections and section titles and numbered section contents (to facilitate cataloging of selected detail drawings) are listed below:

A — MISCELLANEOUS INFORMATION
1000. List of Drawings
2000. Location Map
3000. Key Plan
4000. Project Drafting Standards and Symbols
5000. Miscellaneous

B — SITE PLAN AND DETAILS
1000. Site Plans
2000. Site Details
3000. Test Boring Data
4000. Miscellaneous

C — SMALL SCALE PLANS
1000. Foundation Plans
2000. Floor Plans
3000. Roof Plans
4000. Miscellaneous

D — EXTERIOR ELEVATIONS
1000. Exterior Elevations
2000. Partial Exterior Elevations
3000. Miscellaneous

E — SMALL SCALE SECTIONS THROUGH BUILDING
1000. Longitudinal Sections
2000. Transverse Sections
3000. Partial Sections
4000. Miscellaneous

F — BUILDING CONSTRUCTION DETAILS
1000. Roof-Wall Sections
2000. Floor-Wall Sections
3000. Roof Sections
4000. Floor Sections
5000. Wall Vertical Sections
6000. Wall Plan Sections
7000. Column Plan Sections
8000. Miscellaneous

G — STAIR SECTIONS AND DETAILS
1000. Detail Stair Plans
2000. Stair Sections
3000. Stair Details
4000. Miscellaneous

H — ENTRANCE AND STOREFRONT DETAILS
1000. Detail Entrance Plans
2000. Detail Entrance Elevations
3000. Entrance Details
4000. Detail Storefront Plans
5000. Detail Storefront Elevations
6000. Storefront Details
7000. Miscellaneous

J — WINDOW DETAILS AND CURTAIN WALL DETAILS
1000. Window Types
2000. Window Details
3000. Curtain Wall Details
4000. Miscellaneous

K — DOOR DETAILS
1000. Door Types
2000. Door Frame Details
3000. Threshold Details
4000. Miscellaneous

L — INTERIOR ELEVATIONS
1000. Interior Elevations
2000. Miscellaneous

M — MISCELLANEOUS DETAIL PLANS
1000. Detail Floor Plans
2000. Finish Flooring Plans
3000. Reflected Ceiling Plans
4000. Miscellaneous

N — INTERIOR DETAILS
1000. Millwork Details
2000. Cabinetwork Details
3000. Partition Details
4000. Base Details
5000. Ceiling Details
6000. Miscellaneous

O — MISCELLANEOUS DETAILS
1000. Miscellaneous details are details of building components, building elements, building features, or equipment not included in the other 15 sections. They may include details of such items as skylights, fireplaces, and tackboards.

P — CONVEYING SYSTEMS
1000. Detail Elevator Shaft Plans
2000. Elevator Details
3000. Detail Dumbwaiter Shaft Plans
4000. Dumbwaiter Details
5000. Detail Escalator Plans
6000. Escalator Details
7000. Miscellaneous

Q — SCHEDULES (ARCHITECTURAL)
1000. Architectural Project Schedules
    1000. Room Finish Schedules
    1100. Door Schedules
    1200. Loose Lintel Schedules
    1300. Miscellaneous Schedules

Q — SCHEDULES (NONARCHITECTURAL)
2000. Structural Project Schedules
3000. Heating and Ventilation Project Schedules
4000. Plumbing Project Schedules
5000. Electrical Project Schedules
6000. Civil Project Schedules
7000. Landscaping Project Schedules
8000. Equipment Project Schedules
9000. Composite and Miscellaneous Project Schedules

Q — SCHEDULES (MISCELLANEOUS)
10000. Architectural Office Schedules
11000. Miscellaneous Office Schedules
12000. Building Industry Schedules
13000. Miscellaneous Schedules

| 11 | OFFICE ARCHITECTURAL DRAFTING STANDARDS AND SYMBOLS | DRAWING SCALES AND DRAWING CONTENTS | |

GENERAL

Drawings of different scales are required to explain building design and construction in a practical, comprehensible, and readable manner. Drawings in a set of architectural working drawings consist of small scale general drawings that scale from 1/16" = 1'-0" to 1/4" = 1'-0", small scale detail drawings that scale from 1/16" = 1'-0" to 1/2" = 1'-0", and large scale detail drawings that scale over 1/2" = 1'-0" to full size. Drawing scales most commonly used are: 1/16" = 1'-0", 1/8" = 1'-0", 1/4" = 1'-0", 1/2" = 1'-0", 3/4" = 1'-0", 1½" = 1'-0", 3" = 1'-0", 1/2 FS (1/2 full size), and FS (full size).

Small scale general drawings are primary drawings that consist of plans, elevations, horizontal (or plan) sections, and vertical sections. They include Site Plans, Foundation Plans, Floor Plans, Roof Plans, Exterior Elevations, and Small Scale Sections Through Building. All small scale general drawings mentioned, except Foundation Plans and Roof Plans, are normally included in a set of architectural working drawings; Foundation Plans and Roof Plans are included if they are required to explain design and construction. Small scale general drawings are basically layout drawings that invariably require clarification and amplification by detail drawings and schedules.

Small scale detail drawings are complementary drawings that consist of plans, elevations, horizontal (or plan) sections, and vertical sections. They include Detail Stair Plans, Stair Sections, Detail Entrance Plans, Detail Entrance Elevations, Detail Storefront Plans, Detail Storefront Elevations, Window Types, Door Types, Interior Elevations, Detail Floor Plans, Finish Flooring Plans, Reflected Ceiling Plans, Detail Elevator Shaft Plans, Detail Dumbwaiter Shaft Plans, and Detail Escalator Plans. Some or all small scale detail drawings mentioned are included in a set of architectural working drawings depending on many factors, including extent of professional service, and type, complexity, size, and quality of building construction project.

Large scale detail drawings are complementary drawings that consist of plans, elevations, horizontal (or plan) sections, vertical sections, isometric drawings, and oblique drawings. They include Site Details, Roof-Wall Sections, Floor-Wall Sections, Roof Sections, Floor Sections, Wall Vertical Sections, Wall Plan Sections, Column Plan Sections, Stair Details, Entrance Details, Storefront Details, Window Details, Curtain Wall Details, Door Frame Details, Threshold Details, Millwork Details, Cabinetwork Details, Partition Details, Base Details, Ceiling Details, Miscellaneous Details, Elevator Details, Dumbwaiter Details, and Escalator Details. Some or all large scale detail drawings mentioned are included in a set of architectural working drawings depending on many factors, including extent of professional service, quality of design; and type, construction, and cost of building construction project.

Large scale detail drawings consist primarily of horizontal section and vertical section detail drawings. Horizontal section details normally show construction of supporting building components at corners, at intersections with other supporting building components, and at openings in supporting building components. Vertical section detail drawings normally show construction at ends of supporting and spanning building components, at intersections of supporting building components with spanning building components, and at openings in supporting and spanning building components. Vertical section detail drawings are normally more complicated and more essential to explanation of design and construction than horizontal section detail drawings.

Do not make large scale detail drawings overly explicit. Thin finish flooring, base, wainscot, wall, and ceiling materials that are incidental to building construction, such as vinyl flooring, topset vinyl bases, and fabric or plastic wall and ceiling coverings need not be explicitly shown on some section detail drawings, such as floor-wall section detail drawings that are concerned primarily with rough construction work. Dashed lines representing thin finish flooring and base materials may be shown on these drawings accompanied by a note instructing the reader to "See room finish schedule for finish materials, if any." In vertical section and plan section large scale detail drawings, do not show items beyond section plane in elevation or plan view unless graphic representations are essential to understanding or explanation of section drawings. For example, in door and window head, sill, jamb, vertical mullion, and horizontal mullion large scale detail drawings, do not show frame, wall, sill, stool, or threshold lines in elevation or plan view unless required. This procedure generalizes detail drawings and enables them to apply to more conditions.

Prepare drawings at the smallest scale practical. Small scale general drawings, excluding site plans, normally scale 1/8" = 1'-0" or 1/4" = 1'-0". Detail plans and detail elevations, including interior elevations, normally scale 1/4" = 1'-0". Building construction details and stair details normally scale 1½" = 1'-0" or 3" = 1'-0". Window, curtain wall, door frame, entrance, and storefront details normally scale 3" = 1'-0" and occasionally scale 1½"=1'-0". Window types and door types are normally drawn at the exact or approximate scale of 1/4" = 1'-0" with "not to scale" statement in drawing titles.

Larger scale drawings are more detailed graphically than smaller scale drawings with identical content. For example, in detail section drawings that scale under 3/4" = 1'-0", brickwork in walls is normally indicated by brick material indication in section only. In detail section drawings that scale 3/4" = 1'-0" and over, brickwork in walls is normally indicated by individual brick lines and mortar joint lines with brick and mortar material indications in section.

Window detail drawings for punched opening windows referenced from the window reference symbol normally consist of head, sill, jamb, and vertical mullion detail drawings. Horizontal mullion details are seldom required since they do not affect ceiling, wall, floor, or column construction. For arrangements for window detail drawings on drawing sheets, see Chapter 26.

Curtain wall detail drawings referenced from the section cut symbol consist of some or all of the following: head, jamb, vertical mullion, vertical panel joint, horizontal mullion, horizontal panel joint, spandrel, and sill detail drawings.

Door frame detail drawings referenced from the door reference symbol normally consist of jamb; or head and jamb; or head, sill, and jamb; or head, sill, jamb, and vertical mullion detail drawings. Where more detailed information is required, use the schedule method of door referencing. Where less detailed information is required, use the direct reference method of door referencing. Use only one method of door referencing in a set of working drawings. For arrangements for door frame detail drawings on drawing sheets, see Chapter 26.

Do not indicate graphically mechanical and electrical equipment and detailed structural work in architectural working drawings, unless graphic representations are required to clarify building design or construction. For example, plumbing fixtures are shown in small scale floor plans (and located horizontally by dimensions on floor plans that scale 1/4" = 1'-0" and over) to relate affected construction, such as toilet partitions, plumbing walls, and sink counters to plumbing fixtures. Plumbing vents are not normally shown in exterior elevations, since they do not significantly affect design or construction. Reinforcing bars are not shown in concrete walls, beams, and slabs, since they are indicated in structural drawings.

Most drawings in a set of architectural working drawings are orthographic drawings that show only two dimensions of three dimensional objects. Plans and plan sections show width and depth. Elevations and vertical sections show height and width or height and depth. Several complementary two dimensional orthographic drawings are normally required to explain design and construction of buildings and building elements resulting in redundant drawings.

To control redundancy in a set of architectural working drawings, presentation and dimensioning of some building components shown in small scale general drawings and in some small scale detail drawings must be closely coordinated. These drawings include site plans, foundation plans, floor plans, roof plans, exterior elevations, small scale sections through building, stair sections, interior elevations, detail floor plans, finish flooring plans, and reflected ceiling plans. Dimensioning of these drawings is discussed in Chapter 23. Scales and contents of these drawings are discussed in this chapter.

SITE PLANS

Site plans are based on survey drawings. They are essentially plan views of intended completed building sites that show buildings, site work, and finish grade elevations. Site plans are used primarily to locate horizontally and position vertically buildings, site improvements, and service extensions of public utilities on sites; and to reference site details.

Most graphic information on site plans is shown in plan view, except new buildings, existing buildings to remain, trees, power and/or telephone poles, and other high man-made structures are shown in plan section. Building perimeter lines are normally foundation wall lines at grade. Building walls and partitions are not indicated on site plans. Building roof lines are not indicated on site plans unless they are required to clarify drawings; in which case, they are indicated by dashed lines.

Service extensions of public utilities to buildings; namely, water mains, sanitary sewers, storm sewers (or combined sewers), telephone lines, power lines, and gas mains are shown on site plans. Bench marks (numbers and elevations); test borings (numbers); finish grade, walk, and pavement elevations (by contour lines and/or spot elevations); fire hydrants; manholes, catch basins, and curb inlets (with invert elevations at inlets and outlets, and rim elevations at top covers); fences; contract limit lines; property lines; and other required site information are also shown on site plans.

For small and medium projects, only one site plan (composite drawing) is normally required. For large or complicated projects, more than one site plan may be required to show site work in a practical, comprehensible, and readable manner. Site Demolition Plan (that shows existing structures to be demolished or removed), Site Improvement Plan (that shows and describes buildings and other site improvements, and locates them horizontally), Grading Plan (that indicates existing and new grades and that shows and positions vertically buildings and other site improvements), Utilities Plan, and Planting Plan may be required to explain the site work on a large or complicated project.

Site plans are drawn at different scales, depending on size and complexity of building construction projects and extent of site work. For small and medium projects, usual scales are 1/8'' = 1' -0'', 1'' = 10', 1'' = 20', or 1'' = 30'. For large or complicated projects, usual scales are 1"= 40', 1'' = 50', or 1'' = 60'. Drafting symbols normally or often shown on site plans include site plan symbols, elevation mark symbol, section cut symbol, and section point symbol.

FOUNDATION PLANS

Architectural foundation plans are plan views of intended completed foundation construction that show foundations immediately before backfilling and superstructure construction operations begin. They show such substructure building components in plan view as foundation walls, wall footings, column footings, grade beams (that span between pile caps), pile caps, and piles, and such substructure building components in plan section as crawl space columns. Basement columns and first floor columns are not shown on architectural foundation plans. Basement columns are shown in plan section on basement plans. First floor columns are shown in plan section on first floor plans.

Architectural foundation plans are used primarily to locate horizontally and size horizontally foundation walls and grade beams, and ledges, pockets, and recesses at tops of foundation walls and grade beams; to locate horizontally crawl space columns; to locate vertically tops of foundation walls and grade beams, and ledges, pockets, and recesses at tops of foundation walls and grade beams; and to locate vertically bottoms of wall footings if required to clarify drawings. Bottoms of exterior wall footings are normally located vertically on exterior elevations. Architectural foundation plans are also used to reference architectural foundation details.

Plan view architectural foundation plans may not be required for buildings with cast-in-place concrete exterior walls and cast-in-place concrete foundation walls or grade beams, or for buildings with tops of foundation walls or grade beams that are level and without ledges, pockets, and recesses. For such buildings, plan section structural foundation plans usually contain required architectural foundation plan information.

Structural foundation plans are plan sections of intended completed foundation construction that show foundations immediately before backfilling and superstructure construction operations begin. They show such substructure building components in plan view as wall footings, column footings, pile caps, and piles, and such substructure building components in plan section as foundation walls, grade beams (that span between pile caps), crawl space columns, and basement columns.

Structural foundation plans are used primarily to locate horizontally and size horizontally wall footings, column footings, pile caps, piles, foundation walls, grade beams, crawl space columns, and basement columns; to locate vertically tops of pile caps and tops of column footings; to locate vertically bottoms of wall footings if required to clarify drawings; and to size vertically wall footings, column footings, pile caps, piles, crawl space columns, and basement columns. Structural foundation plans are also used to reference structural foundation details.

Structural foundation plans may be plan view drawings rather than plan section drawings. If they are plan view drawings, architectural foundation plans are not usually required. Horizontal locations and horizontal sizes of ledges, pockets, and recesses at tops of foundation walls and grade beams, and vertical locations of tops of foundation walls and grade beams, and ledges, pockets, and recesses at tops of foundation walls and grade beams may be indicated on plan view structural foundation plans.

Architectural and structural foundation plans are drawn at the same scale as small scale floor plans. Drafting symbols normally or often shown on foundation plans include column line symbol, section cut symbol, section point symbol, minor section symbol, and major section symbol. For explanation of linework in foundation plans, see Chapter 5.

FLOOR PLANS

Floor plans, or more precisely, small scale floor plans (that include basement plans) are horizontal sections through intended completed buildings, taken from about 4'-0'' to ceiling height above floor levels. They are used primarily to locate and size horizontally such building components shown in plan section as columns (columns are normally sized on structural drawings only), piers, walls, partitions, and wall and partition openings, especially door and window openings; and such building components shown in plan view as built-in cabinetwork, stairs, ramps, hatches, access panels, elevators, dumbwaiters, and escalators. Finish flooring materials and patterns are not indicated graphically on small scale floor plans. Finish flooring materials are identified in Room Finish Schedules and shown on detail drawings. Finish flooring patterns are shown, if required, on finish flooring plans. Small scale floor plans are also used to reference room information and door details.

Small scale floor plans are drawn at the scale of 1/16'' = 1'-0'', 1/8'' = 1'-0'', or 1/4'' = 1'-0''. They are normally drawn at the scale of 1/8'' = 1'0''. When required, they are prepared at the scale of 1/4'' = 1'-0'' to convey information more precisely and concisely. At this scale finish flooring, finish wall, and finish ceiling materials are indicated graphically on section drawings. Complete material indications in section and the relative large size of drawings that scale 1/4'' = 1'=0'' reduce or eliminate the need for detail floor plans, except finish flooring plans. Floor plans for alteration projects are usually drawn at the scale of 1/4'' = 1'-0''. Small scale floor plans are rarely drawn at the scale of 1/16'' = 1'-0'', since the small scale prevents clear written and graphic presentation of design and construction information. Drafting symbols normally or often shown on small scale floor plans include room reference symbol, stairway reference symbol and stairs direction indication, door reference symbol, column line symbol, loose lintel reference symbol, section cut symbol, section point symbol, minor section symbol, major section symbol, and equipment symbol.

Framing plans are structural plans that complement architectural floor and roof plans. They are plan sections of intended completed slab on grade construction, such as basement floor slabs and first floor slabs, and intended completed floor or roof framing construction above grade taken about 4'-0'' above floor or roof levels. They show structural floor slabs on grade, framing members without separately installed floor or roof decks or slabs, or framing members with monolithically poured floor or roof slabs. Framing plans show such building components in plan view as horizontal or sloped slabs, including stair slabs and ramp slabs; horizontal or sloped framing members, foundation walls, bearing walls, and columns; and such building components in plan section as foundation walls, bearing walls, and columns. Nonbearing walls and partitions are not indicated on framing plans.

Floor framing plans and roof framing plans are used primarily to locate horizontally and size horizontally such supporting building components shown in plan view as foundation walls and bearing walls; to locate horizontally such supporting building components shown in plan view as columns; to locate horizontally and size horizontally such supporting building components shown in plan section as foundation walls and bearing walls; to locate horizontally and size horizontally and vertically such supporting building components shown in plan section as columns; and to locate horizontally and size horizontally and vertically such spanning building components shown in plan view as arches, trusses, girders, beams, joists, and slabs. Framing plans, consisting of floor slab on grade plans, floor framing plans, and roof framing plans are also used to reference structural framing details.

Floor slab on grade plans are normally not drawn unless they are required to show variable floor conditions, such as floor recesses, pits, steps, ramps, or slab grade beams, or unless they are required to show columns immediately above floor slabs.

Loose lintels directly supporting horizontal or inclined framing members are indicated on framing plans. Loose lintels supporting bearing walls above wall openings are not indicated on framing plans. They are indicated on architectural floor plans or in architectural schedules.

For small buildings of simple design and construction, floor and roof framing may be indicated on small scale architectural floor plans rather than on structural framing plans. Arches, trusses, girders, and beams supporting floors or roofs immediately above floors shown on floor plans are indicated graphically by single dashed lines. The lines are not located by dimensions, unless exact locations of structural members are required. Because joists are always closely spaced, they are not indicated graphically on floor plans. Indications would make plans more difficult to read and would detract from more important information shown on plans. Materials and sizes of arches, trusses, girders, beams, and joists are noted. Spanning directions of joists are indicated by lines with directional arrows.

Structural framing plans are normally drawn at the same scale as small scale architectural floor plans. Drafting symbols normally or often shown on framing plans include column line symbol, section cut symbol, section point symbol, minor section symbol, and major section symbol. For explanation of linework in framing plans, see Chapter 5.

ROOF PLANS

Roof plans are plan views of intended completed buildings that show roof contours and roof surfaces. They are used primarily to locate and size horizontally such building components as copings, scuttles, skylights, chimneys, gutters, and scuppers. They are also used to reference roof details not referenced from small scale sections through building or exterior elevations. Roof plans are not included in sets of architectural working drawings unless they are required to explain design and construction. For many projects, necessary roof information is shown and explained collectively on exterior elevations, small scale sections through building, top floor plans, and roof framing plans.

Roof plans are drawn at the same scale as or at half the scale of small scale floor plans. Drafting symbols normally or often shown on roof plans include column line symbol, section cut symbol, section point symbol, minor section symbol, and major section symbol.

EXTERIOR ELEVATIONS

Exterior elevations are exterior views of intended completed buildings. (Visible portions of buildings above grade lines at buildings are shown by continuous lines, and portions of buildings below grade lines at buildings, such as footings, foundation walls, and areaways are shown by

dashed lines.) They are used primarily to locate and size vertically such building components as wall footings, foundation walls, exterior walls, steps, doors, windows, roofs, skylights, and chimneys. They are also used to reference roof details and exterior wall details, particularly window details.

Independent structures relating to buildings, such as retaining walls, fences, and signs are not shown on exterior elevations unless they are necessary to explain drawings. They are normally shown, located horizontally, and sized horizontally on site plans. Separate elevations of these structures are drawn, which indicate vertical dimensions and elevation levels.

Exterior elevations are drawn at the same scale as small scale floor plans. Drafting symbols normally or often shown on exterior elevations include window reference symbol, column line symbol, elevation mark symbol, section cut symbol, section point symbol, minor section symbol, and major section symbol. For explanation of linework in exterior elevations, see Chapter 5.

SMALL SCALE SECTIONS THROUGH BUILDING

Small scale sections through buildings are vertical sections through intended completed buildings in simplified form. They are used primarily to locate and size vertically floors and roofs, to expose critical intersections of floors and walls and roofs and walls, and to expose critical edge conditions at openings in floors and roofs. They show such building elements, features, and variations in section as large wall openings, wall projections, and changes in suspended ceiling heights. They may show such building features in elevation, on sections that scale 1/4" = 1'-0" and over, as large wall openings, nonceiling high partitions, wainscots, cabinetwork, shelves, mirrors, chalkboards, tackboards, and borrowed lights. They are also used to reference building construction details (primarily floor-wall details and roof-wall details).

On sections that scale under 1/4" = 1'-0" floors, walls, partitions, ceilings, building components, and features in elevation are shown in simplified outline form if required to facilitate comprehension of section or if required to relate isolated interior elevations to total building design and construction.

Most floor and roof framing systems are one directional structurally that result in two different deck or slab edge conditions at exterior walls and at floor and roof openings. At least one longitudinal and one transverse section through building are required to explain design and construction of buildings with one directional floor or roof framing systems. Sections are taken through floor and roof decks or slabs with section cutting planes between supporting joists, beams, girders, trusses, or arches that parallel cutting planes. Small scale sections through buildings are not intentionally cut through door and window openings, since the sections are not used to explain door or window installations.

Small scale sections through building are drawn at the same scale as small scale floor plans. Drafting symbols normally or often shown on small scale sections through building include column line symbol, elevation mark symbol, section cut symbol, and section point symbol.

STAIR SECTIONS

Stair sections are partial vertical sections through intended completed buildings at stairs. They are used to locate and size vertically floors and stair landings; to expose intersections of stairs and floors, stairs and stair landings, and stair landings and walls; and to show relationships between risers and treads. They are also used to reference stair details including handrail details and baluster details.

Small scale stair elevations may be substituted for small scale stair sections where possible and where practical. Exterior stairs exposed to clear view can often be explained architecturally in exterior elevations or in isolated small scale stair elevations.

Stair sections or stair elevations are drawn usually at the scale of 1/4" = 1'-0" and occasionally for uncomplicated stair designs at the scale of 1/8" = 1'-0". Drafting symbols normally or often shown on stair sections include column line symbol, elevation mark symbol, section cut symbol, and section point symbol.

INTERIOR ELEVATIONS

Interior elevations are interior views of rooms or spaces that show finish walls and finish partitions. Perimeter lines of elevations coincide with abutting floor, wall, and ceiling lines at or near walls and partitions shown in elevation. Interior elevations are used primarily to locate and size vertically openings in and building features at or on finish walls and partitions, such as large wall openings (except doors and windows referenced and detailed from door reference symbol and window reference symbol), nonceiling high partitions, wainscots, cabinetwork, shelves,

mirrors, chalkboards, tackboards, and borrowed lights. They are also used to reference interior details.

Interior elevations are drawn usually at the scale of 1/4" = 1'-0" and occasionally for complicated wall designs at the scale of 1/2" = 1'-0". Drafting symbols normally or often shown on interior elevations include column line symbol, section cut symbol, and equipment symbol.

DETAIL FLOOR PLANS

Detail floor plans are partial horizontal sections through intended completed buildings taken from about 4'-0" to ceiling height above floor levels. They are used primarily to locate and size horizontally building components shown in plan section and plan view not adequately located or sized in small scale floor plans. They are also used to reference interior details.

Detail floor plans are drawn usually at the scale of 1/4" = 1'-0" and occasionally for complicated room designs at the scale of 1/2" = 1'-0". Drafting symbols normally or often shown on detail floor plans include room reference symbol, stairway reference symbol and stairs direction indication, column line symbol, section cut symbol, room elevation symbol, and equipment symbol.

FINISH FLOORING PLANS

Finish flooring plans are plan views of intended finish flooring. Perimeter lines of plans coincide with abutting wall lines at or near floors. Finish flooring plans are used primarily to locate and size horizontally complicated or ornate finish flooring configurations, designs, patterns, or features. They are also used to reference interior details.

Finish flooring plans are drawn usually at the same scale as small scale floor plans and occasionally for the more complicated flooring designs at the scale of 1/4"=1'-0" or 1/2"=1'-0". Drafting symbols normally or often shown on finish flooring plans include room reference symbol, stairway reference symbol and stairs direction indication, column line symbol, and section cut symbol.

REFLECTED CEILING PLANS

Reflected ceiling plans are mirror plan views of intended finish ceilings that show all construction including such mechanical and electrical features as air diffusers, air grilles, and lighting fixtures. Perimeter lines of plans coincide with abutting wall lines at or near ceilings. Reflected ceiling plans are used primarily to locate and size horizontally complicated or ornate finish ceiling configurations, designs, patterns, or features. They are also used to reference interior details.

Reflected ceiling plans are drawn usually at the same scale as small scale floor plans and occasionally for the more complicated ceiling designs at the scale of 1/4"=1'-0" or 1/2"=1'-0". Drafting symbols normally or often shown on reflected ceiling plans include room reference symbol, stairway reference symbol, column line symbol, and section cut symbol.

| **12** | **OFFICE ARCHITECTURAL DRAFTING STANDARDS AND SYMBOLS** | **FORMS FOR SCHEDULES** | |

GENERAL

Information about finish building materials, finishes on materials, and some manufactured building components or prefabricated units cannot be presented adequately or efficiently with notes and dimensions on drawings. Schedules are required to present such detailed information in an organized comprehensible manner. Schedules are invariably required to present room information, often required to present door information, and sometimes required to present loose lintel information. If practical, use forms for schedules shown in this chapter that are prepared for small-size detail sheets, to present room, door, and loose lintel information. Complete the forms according to instructions in this chapter.

Forms for schedules on small-size detail sheets should contain sheet title block and should be approximately 7" by 10", 10" by 7", 8 7/8" by 14", 14" by 8 7/8", 14" by 20", or 20" by 14". If practical, forms for schedules on large-size working drawing sheets should be identical to forms for schedules on small-size detail sheets, except area for sheet title block should be omitted and area for schedule name should extend to full width of schedule.

See Appendix of book for information concerning the purchase of 8½" by 11" pads of forms for schedules shown in this chapter and other material pertaining to the standard format for working drawings in this book.

Place appropriate word, words, abbreviations, or numbers in "word response" rectangles in schedules. If response is negative, such as "none," "not required," or "not applicable," place a dashed line in the rectangle. Do not leave "word response" rectangles requiring responses blank. Place appropriate symbol in "symbol response" rectangles in schedules. If response is negative, such as "none," "not required," or "not applicable," leave rectangle blank.

RECORD OF ORIGINAL WORKING DRAWINGS SCHEDULE Q10001

NO. - Indicate working drawing sheet numbers.

STARTING DATE - Indicate dates on which working drawing sheets are started.

ESTIMATED % COMPLETED - This heading is divided into 10 rectangles for each working drawing sheet number. Each rectangle represents 10%. Blacken rectangles for each sheet number as required to indicate estimated percentage of completion. Estimate percentage of completion by comparing work actually completed on each working drawing sheet with work to be done, as shown on each corresponding Sheet Layout. (See Chapter 26 for procedure for preparing Sheet Layouts.)

Revise date in sheet title block to correspond with date of revision to estimate. Get copy of schedule for each revision date so that progress can be ascertained by comparing estimated percentages of completion shown on copies.

COMPLETION DATE - Indicate dates on which working drawing sheets are substantially completed, prior to final check.

DRAFTSMAN - Indicate names of draftsmen assigned to working drawing sheets.

HOURS - Indicate estimated hours required to complete working drawing sheets, including final check, after completion of Sheet Layouts. Indicate actual hours required to complete sheets, including final check, after final check.

SCHED Q10001	GRAY & GREEN · ARCHITECTS 2607 OXFORD DRIVE CHAMPAIGN, ILLINOIS 61820		PROJ. NO. 144-71	DATE 8·6·71	SHT NO.
			RECORD OF ORIGINAL WORKING DRAWINGS		I OF I
WORKING DRAWING SHEET				DRAFTSMAN	HOURS
NO.	STARTING DATE	ESTIMATED % COMPLETED	COMPLE- TION DATE		EST.	ACT.
Z1	7·21·71		7·30·71	W. JENKS	4	5
Z2	6·21·71		7·30·71	T. STEIN	28	34
A1	6·24·71		7·30·71	T. STEIN	28	31
A2	6·14·71		7·30·71	T. STEIN	36	38
A3	6·14·71		7·30·71	W. JENKS	28	30
A4	6·18·71		7·30·71	W. JENKS	48	45
A5	6·28·71		7·30·71	T. STEIN	32	36
A6	6·30·71		7·30·71	W. JENKS	28	30
A7	7·8·71		7·30·71	T. STEIN	20	24
S1	6·14·71		7·30·71	L. GAMBAIANI	32	34
S2	6·24·71		7·30·71	L. GAMBAIANI	32	36
P1					–	–
P2					–	–
H1					–	–
E1					–	–
		See Chapter 26 for other examples of completed Schedule Q10001.				
					316	343
					100%	109%

ROOM FINISH SCHEDULE Q1003

NO. - Indicate room numbers from small scale floor plans.

NAME - Indicate exact room names from small scale floor plans.

FLOOR-BASES-WALLS-CEILING-TRIM- In the 20 vertical columns directly below floor-bases-walls-ceiling-trim headings, indicate project finish room materials, such as vinyl asbestos tile, vinyl tile, plaster, acoustic tile, or wood. Indicate finish floor materials to the left followed by finish bases, walls, ceiling, and trim materials, leaving blank columns between the five groups if possible. Connect groups of finish room materials to appropriate headings by drawing four short vertical or slanted (nonintersecting) lines from long vertical column lines separating groups to four short vertical lines separating headings. Use symbols in legend at upper right hand corner of schedule to indicate either room materials or room materials and finishes. Use either Not Applicable and Applicable symbols, or Not Applicable, Unfinished, Finished, Finished: Paint, and Finished:S&V symbols. If Not Applicable and Applicable symbols are used, blacken or X out the rectangle containing the other four symbols. If Not Applicable, Unfinished, Finished, Finished:Paint, and Finished:S&V symbols are used, blacken or X out the rectangle containing the Applicable symbol.

CLG HT - Indicate room ceiling heights in feet and inches. If room has varied ceiling heights, indicate average ceiling height, such as 10'-0" AVG, or place a dashed line in the rectangle.

DET SHT - Indicate sheet number or numbers on which room interior elevations are presented, such as A9.

REMARKS - Indicate additional room information as required. Wainscot, column, and casework or cabinetwork information is normally included under remarks.

NOTE:
Use Room Finish Schedule Q1003 on projects that have a limited number of different project room materials and a limited number of different material finishes. If Room Finish Schedule Q1003 is inappropriate for a particular project, use Room Finish Schedule Q1001 or Q1002, or devise an appropriate schedule to suit project.

If it is unnecessary to list each room number and room name in a room finish schedule, designate room materials or room materials and finishes directly on small scale floor plans. After room numbers in room reference symbols on small scale floor plans, suffix a letter from Room No. column in Schedule Q1003 (identifying a group of floor, bases, walls, ceiling, and trim materials or materials and finishes) that represents proposed room materials or room materials and finishes. In the Room Name rectangle in the upper left hand corner of the schedule place the following note:

Note:
Room materials are identified by matching letters after room numbers in room reference symbols on small scale floor plans with letters in Room No. column in this schedule.

NO.	NAME	CLG HT	DET SHT
101	NARTHEX-BAPTISTRY	–	A6
102	CLOSET	8'-0"	–
103	STORAGE	7'-11¼"	–
104	CONFESSIONAL	7'-11¼"	–
105	MAIN NAVE	–	A6
106	WEST NAVE	–	–
107	EAST NAVE	–	–
108	SANCTUARY	–	A6
109	CORRIDOR	8'-11½"	–
110	CORRIDOR	8'-11½"	–
111	WORK SACRISTY	8'-11½"	A6
112	WOMEN'S TOILET	8'-11½"	A2,A6

ROOM FINISH SCHEDULE (B)

SCHED Q1003 B — PROJ. NO. / DATE / SHT NO.

	ROOM	FLOOR					BASES		WALLS			CEILING		TRIM		LEGEND		
NO.	NAME	CONCRETE	EXPOSED AGGREGATE CONC	WOOD	VINYL ASBESTOS TILE	CARPET	BRICK	CONCRETE BLOCK	VINYL TILE	BRICK	CONCRETE BLOCK	WOOD	ACOUSTIC TILE	WOOD	METAL	CLG HT	DET SHT	REMARKS
101	NARTHEX-BAPTISTRY		F					U			U	S		S		–	A6	
102	CLOSET		F					P			P	S		S		8'-0"	–	
103	STORAGE				U				F	P	P	U		S		7'-11¼"	–	
104	CONFESSIONAL				U				F	P	P			S		7'-11¼"	–	
105	MAIN NAVE				U	U					U	S		S		–	A6	
106	WEST NAVE				U	U					U	S		S		–	–	
107	EAST NAVE				U	U					U	S		S		–	–	
108	SANCTUARY			S	U	U					U	S		S		–	A6	
109	CORRIDOR					F			F	P	P	S		S		8'-11½"	–	
110	CORRIDOR					F			F	P	P	S		S		8'-11½"	–	
111	WORK SACRISTY					F			F	P		P		S		8'-11½"	A6	
112	WOMEN'S TOILET					F			F	P		P		S		8'-11½"	A2,A6	

Legend: ☐ NOT APPLICABLE / U UNFINISHED / F FINISHED / P FINISHED: PAINT / S FINISHED: S&V — SEE SPECS FOR FINISHES

ROOM FINISH SCHEDULE (C)

SCHED Q1003 C — PROJ. NO. / DATE / SHT NO.

NOTE: Room materials are identified by matching letters after room numbers in room reference symbols on small scale floor plans with letters in Room No. column in this schedule.

	ROOM	FLOOR					BASES		WALLS			CEILING		TRIM		LEGEND		
NO.	NAME	CONCRETE	EXPOSED AGGREGATE CONC	WOOD	VINYL ASBESTOS TILE	CARPET	BRICK	CONCRETE BLOCK	VINYL TILE	BRICK	CONCRETE BLOCK	WOOD	ACOUSTIC TILE	WOOD	METAL	CLG HT	DET SHT	REMARKS
A																–	–	
B																–	–	
C																–	–	
D																–	–	
E																–	–	
F																–	–	
G																–	–	

Legend: ☐ APPLICABLE / ■ NOT APPLICABLE — SEE SPECS FOR FINISHES

ROOM FINISH SCHEDULE (D)

SCHED Q1003 D — PROJ. NO. / DATE / SHT NO.

NOTE: Room materials are identified by matching letters after room numbers in room reference symbols on small scale floor plans with letters in Room No. column in this schedule.

	ROOM	FLOOR					BASES		WALLS			CEILING		TRIM		LEGEND		
NO.	NAME	CONCRETE	EXPOSED AGGREGATE CONC	WOOD	VINYL ASBESTOS TILE	CARPET	BRICK	CONCRETE BLOCK	VINYL TILE	BRICK	CONCRETE BLOCK	WOOD	ACOUSTIC TILE	WOOD	METAL	CLG HT	DET SHT	REMARKS
A			F					U			U	S		S		–	–	
B			F					P			P	S		S		–	–	
C					U				F	P	P	U		S		–	–	
D					U	U					U	S		S		–	–	
E				S	U	U					U	S		S		–	–	
F						F			F	P	P	S		S		–	–	
G						F			F	P		P		S		–	–	

Legend: ☐ NOT APPLICABLE / U UNFINISHED / F FINISHED / P FINISHED: PAINT / S FINISHED: S&V — SEE SPECS FOR FINISHES

ROOM FINISH SCHEDULES Q1001 and Q1002

NO. - Indicate room numbers from small scale floor plans.

NAME - Indicate exact room names from small scale floor plans.

MATL - Indicate finish room materials, such as V.A.T., V.T., PL, AC T, or WD.

FIN. (SCHEDULE Q1001) - Indicate material finishes above lines, such as P, S&V, and W. Indicate exact materials or colors of finishes below lines, such as 2803 (manufacturer's V.A.T. number) or Y-2 (yellow color number two from project color chart). Information below lines is usually added to schedules during the construction phase of service.

FIN. (SCHEDULE Q1002) - Indicate material finishes, such as P, S&V, and W.

CLG HT - Indicate room ceiling heights in feet and inches. If room has varied ceiling heights, indicate average ceiling height, such as 10'-0" AVG, or place a dashed line in the rectangle.

DET SHT - Indicate sheet number or numbers on which room interior elevations are presented, such as A9.

REMARKS - Indicate additional room information as required. Wainscot, column, and casework or cabinetwork information is normally included under remarks.

NOTE:
Use Room Finish Schedule Q1001 or Q1002 on projects that have many different project room materials and material finishes. Use Room Finish Schedule Q1001 on projects where it is required or desirable to indicate exact materials or colors of finishes on drawings. If Room Finish Schedule Q1001 or Q1002 are inappropriate for a particular project, use Room Finish Schedule Q1003, or devise an appropriate schedule to suit project.

SCHED Q1001 — ROOM FINISH SCHEDULE

NO.	NAME	FLOOR MATL	FLOOR FIN.	BASES MATL	BASES FIN.	WALLS MATL	WALLS FIN.	CEILING MATL	CEILING FIN.	TRIM MATL	TRIM FIN.	CLG HT	DET SHT	REMARKS
101	NARTHEX-BAPTISTRY	CONC	−	BR	STV	BR	STV	WD	S&V / SAND	WD	S&V / WAL.	−	A6	EXPOSED AGGREGATE CONC FLOOR SLAB
102	CLOSET	CONC	−	C BL	P / DS	C BL	P / DS	WD	S&V / SAND	WD	S&V / WAL.	8'-0"	−	EXPOSED AGGREGATE CONC FLOOR SLAB
103	STORAGE	CAR.	GOLD	V.T.	KC-2	C BL BR	P / DS	AC T	307	WD	S&V / WAL.	7'-11¼"	−	
104	CONFESSIONAL	CAR.	GOLD	V.T.	KC-2	C BL BR	P / DS	AC T	307	WD	S&V / WAL.	7'-11¼"	−	
105	MAIN NAVE	CAR.	GOLD	BR	STV	BR	STV	WD	S&V / SAND	WD	S&V / WAL.	−	A6	
106	WEST NAVE	CAR.	GOLD	BR	STV	BR	STV	WD	S&V / SAND	WD	S&V / WAL.	−	−	

SCHED Q1002 — ROOM FINISH SCHEDULE

NO.	NAME	FLOOR MATL	FLOOR FIN.	BASES MATL	BASES FIN.	WALLS MATL	WALLS FIN.	CEILING MATL	CEILING FIN.	TRIM MATL	TRIM FIN.	CLG HT	DET SHT	REMARKS
101	NARTHEX-BAPTISTRY	CONC		BR		BR		WD	S&V	WD	S&V	−	A6	EXPOSED AGGREGATE CONC FLOOR SLAB
102	CLOSET	CONC		C BL	P	C BL	P	WD	S&V	WD	S&V	8'-0"	−	EXPOSED AGGREGATE CONC FLOOR SLAB
103	STORAGE	CAR.	−	V.T.	−	C BL BR	P	AC T	−	WD	S&V	7'-11¼"	−	
104	CONFESSIONAL	CAR.	−	V.T.	−	C BL BR	P	AC T	−	WD	S&V	7'-11¼"	−	
105	MAIN NAVE	CAR.	−	BR	−	BR	−	WD	S&V	WD	S&V	−	A6	
106	WEST NAVE	CAR.	−	BR	−	BR	−	WD	S&V	WD	S&V	−	−	
107	EAST NAVE	CAR.	−	BR	−	BR	−	WD	S&V	WD	S&V	−	−	
108	SANCTUARY	CAR. WD	S&V	BR	−	BR	−	WD	S&V	WD	S&V	−	A6	
109	CORRIDOR	V.A.T.	−	V.T.	−	C BL BR	P	WD	S&V	WD	S&V	8'-11½"	−	
110	CORRIDOR	V.A.T.	−	V.T.	−	C BL BR	P	WD	S&V	WD	S&V	8'-11½"	−	
111	WORK SACRISTY	V.A.T.	−	V.T.	−	C BL	P	WD	P	WD	S&V	8'-11½"	A6	
112	WOMEN'S TOILET	V.A.T.	−	V.T.	−	C BL	P	WD	P	WD	S&V	8'-11½"	A2,A6	
113	MEN'S TOILET	V.A.T.	−	V.T.	−	C BL	P	WD	P	WD	S&V	8'-11½"	A2,A6	
114	PRIESTS' SACRISTY	V.A.T.	−	V.T.	−	C BL	P	WD	S&V	WD	S&V	8'-11½"	A6	
115	CLOSET	V.A.T.	−	V.T.	−	C BL	P	WD	S&V	WD	S&V	8'-11½"	−	
116	STORAGE	V.A.T.	−	V.T.	−	C BL	P	WD	S&V	WD	S&V	8'-11½"	−	
117	FURNACE ROOM	CONC	−	C BL	−	C BL	−	WD	S&V	MET	P	−	−	
201	DEAD STORAGE	WD	−	C BL	−	C BL	−	WD	S&V	WD	−	−	−	
202	DEAD STORAGE	WD	−	C BL	−	C BL	−	WD	S&V	WD	−	−	−	

DOOR SCHEDULES Q1101 AND Q1102

NO. - Indicate door numbers from small scale floor plans.

TYPE - Indicate door type letters from elevations of door types.

W - Indicate door dimension widths in feet and inches. For a pair of doors, indicate "2-" before door dimension width.

HT - Indicate door dimension heights in feet and inches.

T - Indicate door thicknesses in inches.

CON. - Indicate door constructions, such as HC, HM, MC, or SC.

DOOR MATL - Indicate door materials, such as GL, MET, or WD.

DOOR FIN. (SCHEDULE Q1101) - Indicate material finishes above lines, such as P or S&V. Indicate colors of finishes below lines, such as P-1 (purple color number one from project color chart). Information below lines is usually added to schedules during the construction phase of service.

DOOR FIN. (SCHEDULE Q1102) - Indicate material finishes, such as P or S&V.

DOOR FRAME MATL - Indicate door frame materials, such as MET or WD.

DOOR FRAME FIN. (SCHEDULE Q1101) - Indicate material finishes above lines, such as P or S&V. Indicate colors of finishes below lines, such as G-3 (green color number three from project color chart). Information below lines is usually added to schedules during the construction phase of service.

DOOR FRAME FIN. (SCHEDULE Q1102) - Indicate material finishes, such as P or S&V.

DOOR FRAME DET NO. - Indicate door frame detail number or numbers from door frame details. Numbers may be a single number, such as 1, or 2, or 3, or 12, or a group of numbers, such as 1A, 1B, or 2A, 2B, 2C, 2D, or 3A, 3B, 3C, or 12A, 1B.

LINTEL - Lintel information is normally shown on door frame head detail drawings. If required, indicate additional lintel data, such as loose lintel steel angle sizes or loose lintel marks.

THRESH. - Indicate threshold materials. If thresholds are detailed, indicate threshold detail drawing numbers. Indicate and note thresholds on small scale floor plans with the direct reference method of door referencing. Do not indicate thresholds on small scale floor plans with the schedule method of door referencing.

HDWE - Indicate hardware group letters (small letters) from specification, if required.

REMARKS - Indicate additional door or door frame information as required. Glass panel and louver information is normally included under remarks.

NOTE:
Use the schedule method of door referencing on projects that require numbering of each door opening to facilitate checking of door and door frame shop drawings and hardware schedules or that require identification of exact materials or colors of finishes on drawings. If Door Schedules Q1101 or Q1102 are inappropriate for a particular project that requires the schedule method of door referencing, devise an appropriate schedule to suit project. Use the direct reference method of door referencing on all other projects. The method of door referencing affects the method of loose lintel sizing. See "Note" in instructions for completing Loose Lintel Schedule in this chapter.

SCHED Q1101

DOOR SCHEDULE

| | | | | | | | | | | | | | PROJ. NO. | DATE | SHT NO. |

		DOOR					DOOR FRAME			LINTEL	THRESH.	HDWE SEE SPECS	REMARKS
NO.	TYPE	W	HT	T	CON.	MATL	FIN.	MATL	FIN.	DET NO.			
101	F	2-3'-0"	7'-0"	2¼"	SC	WD	S&V CHAR.	WD	S&V WAL.	3-A3	-	BRONZE	-

SCHED Q1102

DOOR SCHEDULE

| | | | | | | | | | | | | | PROJ. NO.: | DATE | SHT NO. |

		DOOR					DOOR FRAME			LINTEL	THRESH.	HDWE SEE SPECS	REMARKS
NO.	TYPE	W	HT	T	CON.	MATL	FIN.	MATL	FIN.	DET NO.			
101	F	2-3'-0"	7'-0"	2¼"	SC	WD	S&V	WD	S&V	3-A3	-	BRONZE	-
102	F	2-3'-0"	7'-0"	2¼"	SC	WD	S&V	WD	S&V	1-A3	-	BRONZE	-
103	A	3'-0"	7'-0"	1¾"	HC	WD	S&V	WD	S&V	2	-	-	-	UNDERCUT DOOR 1"
104	A	3'-0"	7'-0"	1¾"	HC	WD	S&V	WD	S&V	2	-	-	-	UNDERCUT DOOR 1"
105	C	2-2'-8"	7'-8"	2¼"	SC	WD	S&V	WD	S&V	2	-	-	-	UNDERCUT DOORS 1"
106	C	2-2'-8"	7'-8"	2¼"	SC	WD	S&V	WD	S&V	2	-	-	-	UNDERCUT DOORS 1"

LOOSE LINTEL SCHEDULE Q1201

MARK - Indicate loose lintel marks from small scale floor plans and door schedules, if any.

MATERIAL - Indicate loose lintel materials, such as steel, precast concrete, reinforced concrete block, reinforced clay tile, or wood.

SECTION - Draw vertical sections through lintels at the approximate scale of 1/2'' = 1'-0''. Note, size, and dimension as required.

ROUGH OPENING - Indicate rough opening dimensions in feet and inches.

BEARING AT EACH END - Indicate bearing at each end in inches.

REMARKS - Indicate additional lintel information as required.

NOTE:
Use one or a combination of two or three methods to size loose lintels; namely, in specifications, with notes on small scale plans and detail drawings, and with loose lintel schedule and loose lintel reference symbols on small scale plans and loose lintel marks in door schedules. Do not use the loose lintel reference symbol at doorways on small scale plans with the schedule method of door referencing. If Loose Lintel Schedule Q1201 is inappropriate for a particular project that requires the schedule-symbol method of loose lintel sizing, devise an appropriate schedule to suit project.

SCHED Q1201				PROJ. NO.	DATE	SHT NO.
		LOOSE LINTEL SCHEDULE				
MARK	MATERIAL	SECTION	ROUGH OPENING	BEARING AT EACH END	REMARKS	
L1	STEEL	1/2" — 2 L̄s 6 × 3½ × 5/16	7'-0⅞"	8"		
L2	STEEL	¼" — 2 L̄s 4 × 3½ × 5/16	2'-8⅞"	8"		
L3	STEEL	¼" — 2 L̄s 6 × 3½ × 5/16	7'-0⅞"	8"		
L4	STEEL	1/2" — 3 L̄s 6 × 3½ × 3/8	8'-5"	8"	BOLT 2 L̄s WITH ½"ø BOLTS @ 2'-0" O.C.	
L5	REINFORCED CONC BLOCK	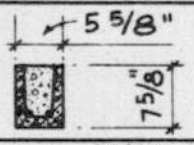 5⅝" — 7⅝" — 2 - #3 REBARS	3'-4"	7¹³/₁₆"	FILL LINTELS WITH CONCRETE	
L6	REINFORCED CLAY TILE	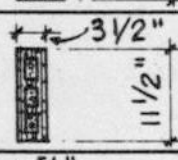 3½" — 11½" — 1 - #3 REBAR	3'-5"	9¼"	FILL LINTELS WITH CONCRETE	
L7	PRECAST CONCRETE	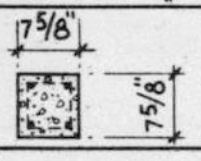 7⅝" — 7⅝" — 4 - #4 REBARS	6'-4"	8"	SPACE STIRRUPS 3" APART	

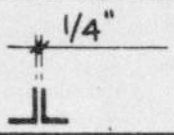

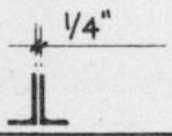

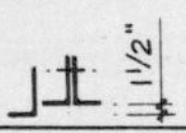

SCHED Q10001			PROJ. NO.:		DATE:		SHT NO.
			RECORD OF ORIGINAL WORKING DRAWINGS				

WORKING DRAWING SHEET						DRAFTSMAN	HOURS	
NO.	STARTING DATE	ESTIMATED % COMPLETED				COMPLE-TION DATE	EST.	ACT.
			PROJ. NO.:		DATE:		SHT NO.

ROOM FINISH SCHEDULE

		DATE:		PROJ. NO.:		SHT NO.

LEGEND

	APPLICABLE
	NOT APPLICABLE
U	UNFINISHED
F	FINISHED
P	FINISHED: PAINT
S	FINISHED: S&V

SEE SPECS FOR FINISHES

ROOM		FLOOR	BASES	WALLS	CEILING	TRIM	CLG HT	DET SHT	REMARKS
NO.	NAME								

SCHED Q1003

ROOM FINISH SCHEDULE

PROJ. NO.: DATE: SHT NO.

SCHED
Q1002

ROOM		FLOOR		BASES		WALLS		CEILING		TRIM		CLG HT	DET SHT	REMARKS
NO.	NAME	MATL	FIN.	MATL	FIN.	MATL	FIN.	MATL	FIN.	MATL	FIN.			

ROOM FINISH SCHEDULE

SCHED Q1001

PROJ. NO.:

DATE:

SHT NO.

ROOM		FLOOR		BASES		WALLS		CEILING		TRIM		CLG HT	DET SHT	REMARKS
NO.	NAME	MATL	FIN.	MATL	FIN.	MATL	FIN.	MATL	FIN.	MATL	FIN.			

DOOR SCHEDULE

SCHED Q1102	PROJ. NO.:	DATE:	SHT NO.

NO.	DOOR						DOOR FRAME			LINTEL	THRESH.	HDWE SEE SPECS	REMARKS
	TYPE	W	HT	T	CON.	MATL	FIN.	MATL	FIN.	DET NO.			

DOOR SCHEDULE

SCHED Q1101

PROJ. NO.:

DATE:

SHT NO.

NO.	DOOR						DOOR FRAME			LINTEL	THRESH.	HDWE SEE SPECS	REMARKS
	TYPE	W	HT	T	CON. MATL	FIN.	MATL	FIN.	DET NO.				

MARK	MATERIAL	SECTION	ROUGH OPENING	BEARING AT EACH END	REMARKS

LOOSE LINTEL SCHEDULE

SCHED Q1201   PROJ. NO.:   DATE: SHT NO.

| 13 | OFFICE ARCHITECTURAL DRAFTING STANDARDS AND SYMBOLS | SHEET SIZES AND TITLE BLOCKS | |

SHEET SIZES

One sheet type is necessary for working drawings; two sheet types are sometimes desirable. Large-size working drawing sheet type is required to accommodate large general drawings. These drawings are normally unique small scale drawings prepared especially for a particular building construction project. Small-size detail sheet type is not required but is particularly suited for schedules and some small detail drawings. These drawings are usually large scale drawings that amplify and explain small scale general drawings and are drawings that could apply to different building construction projects.

For clarity, detail drawings referenced directly from small scale sections through building should be shown with site plan, small scale plans, exterior elevations, small scale sections through building, and stair sections on large-size working drawing sheets. Detail drawings that may be applicable to different projects may be shown, for production economy and reading convenience, on small-size detail sheets (and reused on different projects). Only one large-size working drawing sheet size (preferably a multiple of 11" by 8 1/2") should be used for a particular building construction project. Originals or reproductions of small-size detail sheets should be 11" by 8 1/2" or 11" by (foldable) 16". Depending on number of drawings and specifications, small-size detail sheets may be bound into a separate booklet or bound with specifications.

If practical, use large-size working drawing sheet types D, E, or F with standard title block and small-size detail sheet types A, B, and C with standard title block shown in this chapter.

To reduce drawing production costs, large-size working drawing sheets and small-size detail sheets should be preprinted and sold at local drafting supply stores. Names and addresses of design firms, north arrows, and other constant or repetitive information would be placed in standard title blocks by rubber stamps or by other fast and economical methods. To further reduce drawing production costs and assure graphic communication consistency, project drafting standards and symbols should also be preprinted on a few large-size working drawing

sheets (types E and F) and on a few small-size detail sheets (type A). Also, schedules should be preprinted on 11" by 8 1/2" or 11" by (foldable) 16" sheets.

See Appendix of book for information concerning the purchase of large-size working drawing sheets and small-size detail sheets shown in this chapter, 8½" by 11" pads of project drafting standards and symbols shown in Chapters 16, 17, 18, 19, and 20, 8½" by 11" pads of forms for schedules shown in Chapter 12, and other material pertaining to the standard format for working drawings in this book.

Large-size working drawing sheets are required. They could contain all architectural drawings and schedules or could be limited to the following architectural information:

A. Miscellaneous information (list of large-size working drawing sheet drawings, location map, key plan, and project drafting standards and symbols).
B. Site plan.
C. Small scale plans.
D. Exterior elevations.
E. Small scale sections through building.
F. Building construction details.
G. Stair sections and details.
L. Interior elevations.
M. Miscellaneous detail plans.
O. Miscellaneous details.
P. Conveying systems.

Small-size detail sheets are optional. They could contain all or some of the following architectural information:

A. Miscellaneous information (list of small-size detail sheet drawings and project drafting standards and symbols if not shown on large-size working drawing sheets).
B. Site details and test boring data.
H. Entrance and storefront details.
J. Window details and curtain wall details.
K. Door details.
N. Interior details.
O. Miscellaneous details.
Q. Schedules.

Long dashed lines on small-size detail sheets indicate normal drawing limit lines for one drawing; short dashed lines indicate normal drawing limit lines for more than one drawing; dashed-dotted lines indicate drawing limit lines for one or more than one drawing. For rationale of drawing limit lines, see Schedule of Detail Drawing Sizes on page 121, and Arrangements for Window and Door Frame Detail Drawings on pages 124 and 125.

Use small-size detail sheet type C for half-size reproductions only. Linework, printing, and lettering in title blocks should be twice the size of standards indicated in this book. This sheet type is particularly suited for presenting large scale detail drawings that scale 3"= 1'-0", such as door frame detail drawings and window detail drawings. If applicable, place a note at suitable location on each sheet type C that reads as follows: NOTE: Drawings on this sheet are one-half size reproductions. Drawing scales are one-half size indicated.

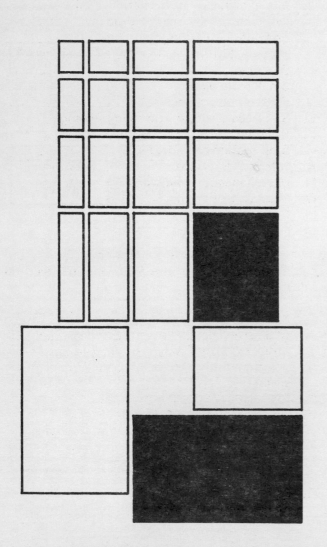

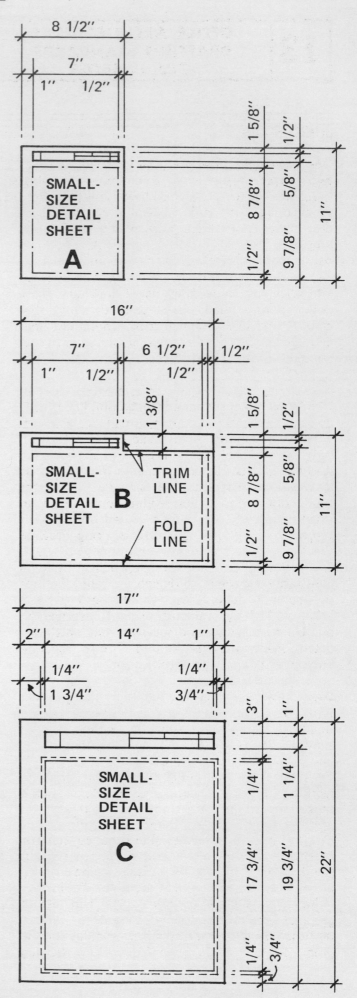

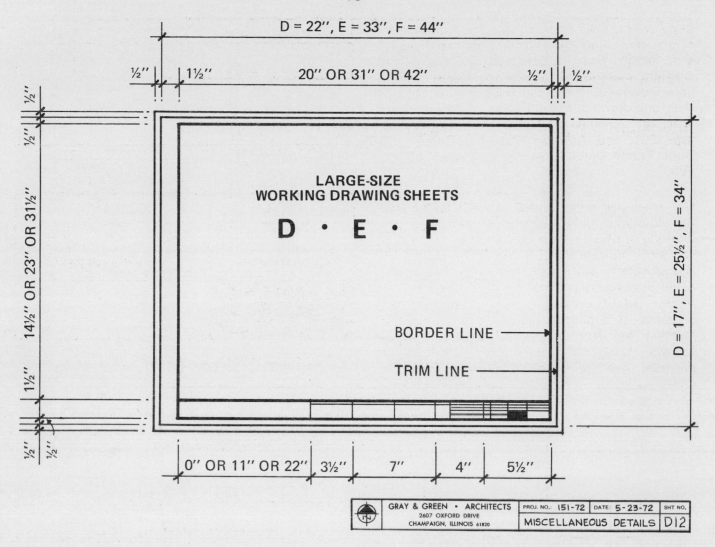

D = 22", E = 33", F = 44"

½"   1½"   20" OR 31" OR 42"   ½" ½"

½

14½" OR 23" OR 31½"

1½"

½" ½"

D = 17", E = 25½", F = 34"

**LARGE-SIZE
WORKING DRAWING SHEETS**

D · E · F

BORDER LINE →

TRIM LINE →

0" OR 11" OR 22" 3½" 7" 4" 5½"

GRAY & GREEN · ARCHITECTS
2607 OXFORD DRIVE
CHAMPAIGN, ILLINOIS 61820
PROJ. NO.: 151-72 DATE: 5-23-72 SHT NO.
MISCELLANEOUS DETAILS D12

STANDARD TITLE BLOCK FOR SMALL - SIZE DETAIL SHEETS

TITLE BLOCKS

Title blocks for required large-size working drawing sheets should contain all necessary information about design firm or firms, owner, project, and drawings. Title blocks for optional small-size detail sheets should contain only selected information about project and drawings, no information about owner, and complete information about appropriate design firm. Assign sheet titles and numbers based on recommendations in Chapter 10.

NO.	REVISION DATE	DATE	PROJECT NO.
1	JULY 14,1972	MAY 23,1972	151-72
		SET NUMBER	SHEET NUMBER
			A 4

NORTH	SCALE:	AS NOTED
	DESIGNED:	F. L. W.
	DRAWN:	J. F. K.
	CHECKED:	L. B. J.
	APPROVED:	R. M. N.

PROJECT NAME, LOCATION, OWNER	SHEET TITLE
ADDITIONS AND ALTERATIONS TO LEWIS OFFICE BUILDING 1236 MOYER STREET CHICAGO, ILLINOIS 60606 SAMUEL G. CLAYTON · OWNER	THIRD FLOOR PLAN AND DETAILS

ARCHITECT

GRAY & GREEN · ARCHITECTS
2607 OXFORD DRIVE
CHAMPAIGN, ILLINOIS 61820
TELEPHONE 217 - 325-0961

STANDARD TITLE BLOCK FOR LARGE - SIZE WORKING DRAWING SHEETS

		PROJ. NO.:	DATE:	SHT NO.

STANDARD TITLE BLOCK FOR SMALL-SIZE DETAIL SHEETS

NO.	REVISION DATE	DATE	PROJECT NO.
		SET NUMBER	SHEET NUMBER

NORTH	SCALE:
	DESIGNED:
	DRAWN:
	CHECKED:
	APPROVED:

PROJECT NAME, LOCATION, OWNER	SHEET TITLE

ARCHITECT

STANDARD TITLE BLOCK FOR LARGE-SIZE WORKING DRAWING SHEETS

| 14 | OFFICE ARCHITECTURAL DRAFTING STANDARDS AND SYMBOLS | MISCELLANEOUS OFFICE DRAFTING STANDARDS AND SYMBOLS | |

Formulate additional office drafting standards and symbols, if required. Devise them to complement standards and symbols shown in Chapters 4 through 13.

| 15 | STANDARD FORMAT FOR ARCHITECTURAL WORKING DRAWINGS | PROJECT ARCHITECTURAL DRAFTING STANDARDS AND SYMBOLS | |

PROJECT ARCHITECTURAL DRAFTING STANDARDS AND SYMBOLS

Uniform Project Architectural Drafting Standards and Symbols are used to produce unambiguous, unified drawings and to reduce confusion in the building industry. They convey information directly and should be understandable to all members of the building industry; consequently, they are shown and explained in each set of architectural working drawings. See illustrations and explanations of Project Architectural Drafting Standards and Symbols in the six chapters listed below:

16 Site Plan Symbols
17 Material Indications in Section
18 Reference Symbols
19 Dimensioning
20 List of Abbreviations
21 Miscellaneous Project Drafting Standards and Symbols

For examples of material indications in section in Section Conventions for Common Interior Partitions and Common Exterior Walls, see Chapter 8. For locations for reference symbols in architectural working drawings, see Chapter 25. For examples of dimensioning in architectural working drawings, see Chapter 23. For applications of abbreviations in schedules, see Chapter 12. Applications of site plan symbols in architectural working drawings are shown in the book *The Site Plan in Architectural Working Drawings* by George T. Clayton, published by Stipes Publishing Company, Champaign, Illinois 61820.

See Appendix of book for information concerning the purchase of 8½" by 11" pads of project drafting standards and symbols shown in Chapters 16, 17, 18, 19, and 20 and other material pertaining to the standard format for working drawings in this book.

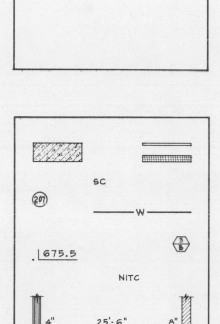

DRAWING PROCESS

See pages 126-127 for systematic incorporation of Project Architectural Drafting Standards and Symbols in drawings and pages 121-125 for drawing arrangements.

| 16 | PROJECT ARCHITECTURAL DRAFTING STANDARDS AND SYMBOLS | SITE PLAN SYMBOLS | |

● BM-1- 680.0   BENCH MARK — NUMBER — ELEVATION IN FEET

◑ TB-1   TEST BORING — NUMBER

. 677.5   EXISTING SPOT ELEVATION TO CHANGE

. 676.0   EXISTING SPOT ELEVATION TO REMAIN

. 675.5   NEW SPOT ELEVATION

677.5 OR 677.5   EXISTING CONTOUR TO CHANGE

676.0   EXISTING CONTOUR TO REMAIN

675.5   NEW CONTOUR

FIRE HYDRANT

○ MH   MANHOLE

○ CB   CATCH BASIN

CURB INLET

POWER AND/OR TELEPHONE POLE

LIGHT STANDARD

◎ 10" DIAM. OAK   EXISTING TREE TO REMAIN

✕ 10" DIAM. OAK   EXISTING TREE TO BE REMOVED

——————W——————   WATER MAIN

——————T——————   TELEPHONE LINE

——————P——————   POWER LINE

————— G —————   GAS MAIN

————— O —————   FUEL OIL LINE

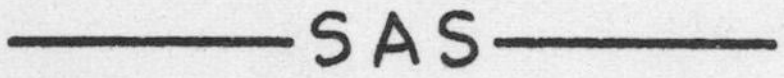

————— SAS —————   SANITARY SEWER

————— STS —————   STORM SEWER

————— COS —————   COMBINED SEWER

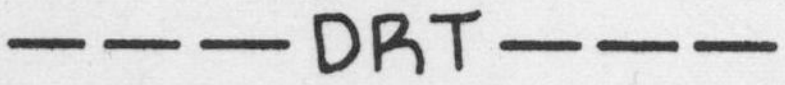

— — — DRT — — —   DRAIN TILE

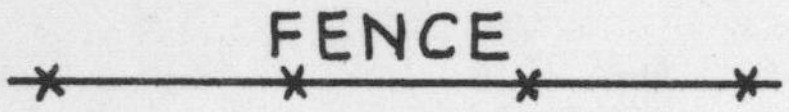

—×— FENCE —×—×—×—   FENCE

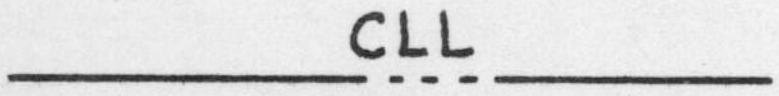

——— CLL ———   CONTRACT LIMIT LINE

——— PRL ———   PROPERTY LINE

NEW BUILDING

EXISTING BUILDING TO REMAIN

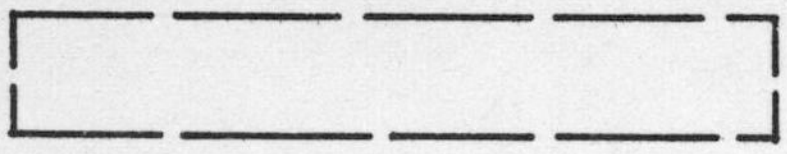

EXISTING BUILDING TO BE REMOVED

NOTE:
Sizes of site plan symbols on drawings may be slightly larger or smaller than shown above to suit scales of site plans.

| 17 | PROJECT ARCHITECTURAL DRAFTING STANDARDS AND SYMBOLS | MATERIAL INDICATIONS IN SECTION | |

Materials in elevation are identified by notes only or by notes and material indications in elevation. Materials in small scale plan and vertical sections and large scale plan and vertical section details are identified by material indications in section shown below, or, if necessary to clarify drawings, by notes and material indications in section shown below. Material indications in section that are similar and contiguous in drawings are invariably noted. Finish flooring, finish wall, and finish ceiling materials are not normally identified by notes in plan sections or vertical sections that scale 1/2″ = 1'-0″ and under. Thin finish flooring, finish wall, and finish ceiling materials less than 7/8″ in total thickness, such as vinyl tile (resilient flooring), plaster, and acoustic tile are not normally indicated by material indications in section in plan sections or vertical sections that

scale under 1/4″ = 1'-0″ because of drafting limitations. Room finish materials are normally identified by room finish schedules and detail drawings.

More than one material indication in section is shown below for some materials. Single indications are used in all drawings. Top indications are normally used in drawings that scale 1/2″ = 1'-0″ and under. Bottom indications are used in drawings that scale over 1/2″ = 1'-0″ and sometimes in drawings that scale 1/2″ = 1'-0″ and under. Side by side indications are selective indications used in drawings that scale over 1/2″ = 1'-0″. Material indications in section will vary slightly on drawings because of different drawing scales or sizes and because of different drafting techniques.

ACOUSTIC TILE

ASBESTOS-CEMENT

BRICK: FACE BRICK

BRICK: COMMON BRICK

BRICK: GLAZED BRICK

BRICK: FIRE BRICK

CARPET

CAULKING

CEMENT

CERAMIC TILE

CLAY TILE

CONCRETE: CAST-IN-PLACE

CONCRETE: PRECAST

CONCRETE: BLOCK

CONCRETE: BRICK

EARTH OR BACKFILL

EXISTING CONSTRUCTION TO REMAIN

EXISTING CONSTRUCTION TO BE REMOVED

EXISTING CONSTRUCTION AT NEW WORK TO BE PATCHED TO MATCH EXISTING CONSTRUCTION

GLASS: SHEET, PLATE, FLOAT

GLASS: STRUCTURAL

GLASS: BLOCK

GRANITE

GRAVEL

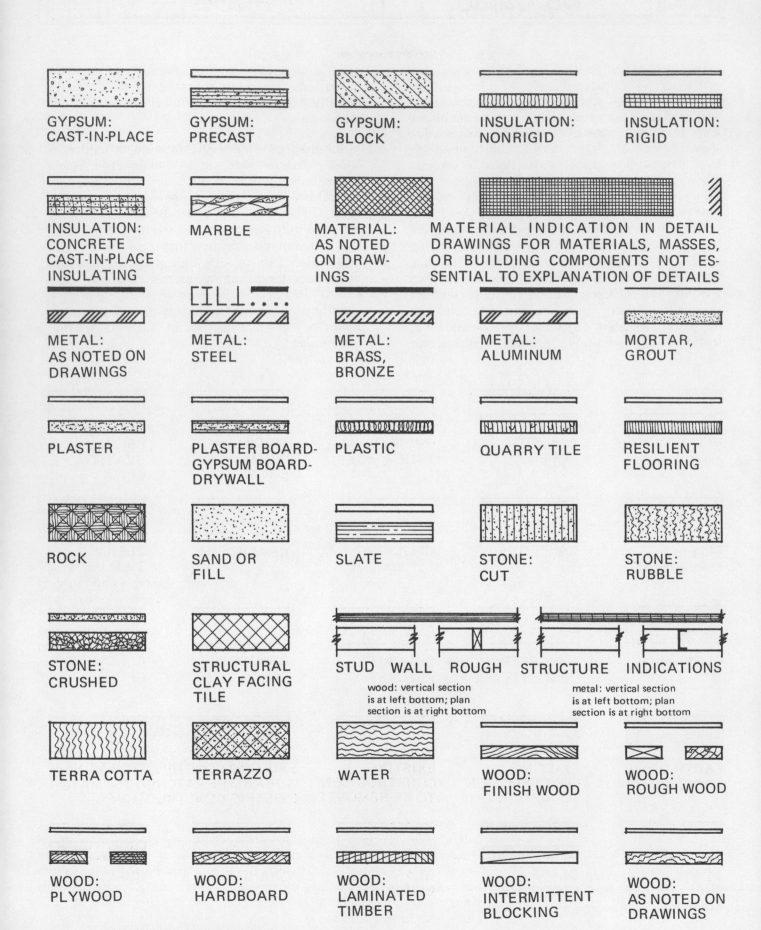

GYPSUM: CAST-IN-PLACE

GYPSUM: PRECAST

GYPSUM: BLOCK

INSULATION: NONRIGID

INSULATION: RIGID

INSULATION: CONCRETE CAST-IN-PLACE INSULATING

MARBLE

MATERIAL: AS NOTED ON DRAWINGS

MATERIAL INDICATION IN DETAIL DRAWINGS FOR MATERIALS, MASSES, OR BUILDING COMPONENTS NOT ESSENTIAL TO EXPLANATION OF DETAILS

METAL: AS NOTED ON DRAWINGS

METAL: STEEL

METAL: BRASS, BRONZE

METAL: ALUMINUM

MORTAR, GROUT

PLASTER

PLASTER BOARD-GYPSUM BOARD-DRYWALL

PLASTIC

QUARRY TILE

RESILIENT FLOORING

ROCK

SAND OR FILL

SLATE

STONE: CUT

STONE: RUBBLE

STONE: CRUSHED

STRUCTURAL CLAY FACING TILE

STUD WALL ROUGH STRUCTURE INDICATIONS

wood: vertical section is at left bottom; plan section is at right bottom

metal: vertical section is at left bottom; plan section is at right bottom

TERRA COTTA

TERRAZZO

WATER

WOOD: FINISH WOOD

WOOD: ROUGH WOOD

WOOD: PLYWOOD

WOOD: HARDBOARD

WOOD: LAMINATED TIMBER

WOOD: INTERMITTENT BLOCKING

WOOD: AS NOTED ON DRAWINGS

| 18 | PROJECT ARCHITECTURAL DRAFTING STANDARDS AND SYMBOLS | REFERENCE SYMBOLS | |

DRAWING REFERENCE SYMBOL

8 - drawing number (on sheet A5)

A5 - sheet number on which drawing is presented (architectural sheet number 5)

8-A5 - indication for drawing number and sheet number on which drawing is presented, in notes, schedules, and specifications.

DOOR REFERENCE SYMBOL - SCHEDULE METHOD

2 - floor number

07 - door opening (on second floor)

207 - door number

See list of drawings for sheet numbers on which door schedules, door types, and door frame details are presented.

DOOR REFERENCE SYMBOL-DIRECT REFERENCE METHOD

D - door type

6 - door frame detail number

b - hardware group letter

See list of drawings for sheet numbers on which door types and door frame details are presented. See specifications for contents of hardware group letter.

WINDOW REFERENCE SYMBOL

B - window type

3 - window detail number

See list of drawings for sheet numbers on which window types and window details are presented.

TITLE REFERENCE SYMBOL

Drawing titles are placed under all drawings, except some building component type drawings, such as door type and window type drawings. Locations of details on building sites or in buildings are sometimes included in detail drawing titles for general referencing purposes only. Do not use information in drawing titles to determine numbers or quantities.

D - door type

6 - door frame detail number*

B - window type

3 - window detail number*

8 - drawing number (on sheet A5)*

A5 - sheet number on which drawing is presented (architectural sheet number 5)

*In some grouped detail drawings, especially door frame detail drawings and window detail drawings, drawing numbers may be suffixed by letters to differentiate detail drawings. For example, window details consisting of head, sill, jamb, vertical mullion, and horizontal mullion detail drawings might be designated 3A, 3B, 3C, 3D, and 3E respectively.

HALL
304

ROOM REFERENCE SYMBOL

HALL - room name
3 - floor number
04 - space number (on third floor)
304 - room number
See room finish schedule for room and stairway materials and finishes, and room detail sheet numbers. See list of drawings for sheet numbers on which room finish schedules are presented.

SRWY
2
UP 16R

STAIRWAY REFERENCE SYMBOL
AND STAIRS DIRECTION INDICATION

SRWY - stairway
2 - stairway number
16R - 16 risers, UP or DN (down) as indicated

7   **G**

COLUMN LINE SYMBOL

7 - column reference line number
G - column reference line letter

ELEVATION MARK SYMBOL

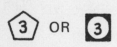

LOOSE LINTEL REFERENCE SYMBOL

LI - loose lintel mark
See list of drawings for sheet numbers on which loose lintel schedules, that contain loose lintel marks, are presented.

3 OR **3**

REVISION SYMBOL

3 - revision number

127

EQUIPMENT SYMBOL

127 — equipment number

NOTE:
Size of drawing reference symbol, contained in section indication symbols on drawings, varies. Sizes of door and window reference symbols on drawings may be slightly larger than shown above to suit scales of small scale general drawings or to accommodate lettering in symbols.

| 19 | PROJECT ARCHITECTURAL DRAFTING STANDARDS AND SYMBOLS | DIMENSIONING | |

Dimensions are indicated in notes and schedules and at dimension lines on drawings. Dimensioning points are indicated on dimension lines at intersections of object lines (that include building component lines, building element lines, and building feature lines), dimension extension lines, and dimension reference lines, by arrowheads, dots, or slashes. Arrowheads and dots are used with modular dimensioning. Slashes are used with regular dimensioning. If required dimensions are not indicated numerically on drawings, they may be obtained by scaling drawings. Verify scaled dimensions with architect before beginning work affected by scaled dimensions. Undesignated size dimensions in notes and schedules are normally arranged in the following order: height, width, and depth.

Actual dimensions and nominal dimensions are indicated on drawings. Actual dimensions are whole and/or fractional numbers (to the nearest 1/16''), such as 1'', 1½'', 7 5/8'', and 10''. Nominal dimensions are whole numbers that are up to 1'' larger than fractional numbers they represent, such as 2'' for 1½'' and 8'' for 7 5/8''. Actual dimensions are normally indicated on drawings that scale over 1/4'' = 1'-0'' for construction accuracy. Actual dimensions, and nominal dimensions for fractional numbers 1½'' and over that size masses, are normally indicated on drawings that scale 1/4'' = 1'-0'' and under, to simplify small scale drawings and to enhance oral communications.

In regular dimensioning with drawings that scale 1/4'' = 1'-0'' and under, size and location dimensions are indicated to rough surfaces, such as to faces of studs or masonry that are structural elements of plastered partitions. If a dimension on a small scale drawing is to a finish surface, the side and material of the surface is noted, such as "face of plaster." Nominal mass dimensions may be indicated in strings of continuous mass-space dimensions, such as strings of horizontal dimensions through partitions (masses) and rooms (spaces) in small scale floor plans. When this dimensioning method is used, masses should be constructed centered between nominal mass dimension lines. For example, a nominal 4'' thick concrete block partition with an actual thickness of 3 5/8'' should be constructed 3/16'' inside nominal 4'' mass dimension lines.

MODULAR DIMENSIONING   NTS

Arrowheads are indicated to 4'' spaced horizontal and vertical grid lines. Dots are indicated off 4'' spaced grid lines.

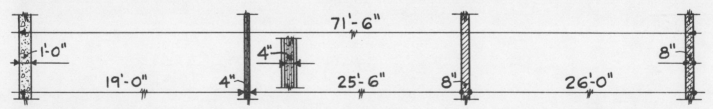

REGULAR DIMENSIONING   NTS

Actual dimensions are normally indicated on drawings that scale over 1/4''=1'-0''. Actual dimensions, and nominal dimensions for fractional numbers 1½'' and over that size masses, are normally indicated on drawings that scale 1/4'' = 1'-0'' and under. Dimensions are to rough surfaces unless indicated or noted otherwise.

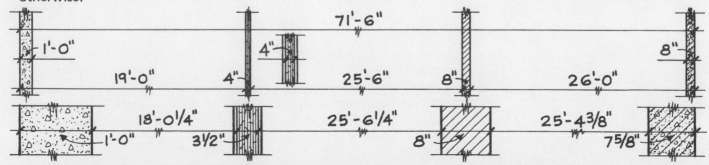

| 20 | PROJECT ARCHITECTURAL DRAFTING STANDARDS AND SYMBOLS | LIST OF ABBREVIATIONS | |

AC P	ACOUSTIC PLASTER	L	LONG, LINE
AC T	ACOUSTIC TILE	LAV	LAVATORY
ACT.	ACTUAL	LINO	LINOLEUM
AL	ALUMINUM	LR	LIVING ROOM
ARCH.	ARCHITECTURAL	LT	LIGHT, LAUNDRY TRAY
A. T.	ASPHALT TILE	MAR	MARBLE
AVG	AVERAGE	MATL	MATERIAL
BL	BLOCK	MAX.	MAXIMUM
BPL	BEARING PLATE	MC	MINERAL CORE
BR	BRICK, BEDROOM	MET	METAL
CAR.	CARPET	MIN.	MINIMUM
CAT.	CATALOG	ML & P	METAL LATH AND PLASTER
C BL	CONCRETE BLOCK	M. O.	MASONRY OPENING
CEM	CEMENT	MULL.	MULLION
CER T	CERAMIC TILE	N. A.	NOT APPLICABLE
CFM	CUBIC FEET PER MINUTE	NAT	NATURAL
C I	CAST IRON	NITC	NOT IN THIS CONTRACT
CL	CENTER LINE	NO., #	NUMBER
CLG	CEILING	NOM.	NOMINAL
CLO	CLOSET	NTS	NOT TO SCALE
CON.	CONSTRUCTION	O. C.	ON CENTER
CONC	CONCRETE	O. D.	OUTSIDE DIMENSION
CONT	CONTINUOUS	P	PAINT
COR	CORRIDOR	PL	PLASTER, PLATE
C PL	CEMENT PLASTER	PLAS T	PLASTIC TILE
C T	CORK TILE	PL BD	PLASTER BOARD
C TO C	CENTER TO CENTER	PLYWD	PLYWOOD
CW	COLD WATER	POL.	POLISHED
DET	DETAIL	PROJ.	PROJECT
DF	DRINKING FOUNTAIN	Q. T.	QUARRY TILE
DIAM.	DIAMETER	R	RISER, RANGE, RADIUS
DIM	DIMENSION	RB	RUBBER
DN	DOWN	REBAR	REINFORCING BAR
DO	DITTO	REF.	REFRIGERATOR, REFERENCE
DR	DINING ROOM, DOOR	REV	REVISION
DS	DOWNSPOUT	RM, RMS	ROOM, ROOMS
DWG	DRAWING	R. O.	ROUGH OPENING
E	ENAMEL, EXHAUST	R. T.	RUBBER TILE
EA	EACH	S	SUPPLY
EL	ELEVATION	S & V	STAIN & VARNISH
ELEV	ELEVATION	SC	SOLID CORE
ENT	ENTRANCE	SCFT	STRUCT CLAY FACING TILE
EST.	ESTIMATED	SCHED	SCHEDULE
E. W.	EACH WAY	SEC	SECTION
EXIST	EXISTING	SHT	SHEET
EXT	EXTERIOR	SPECS	SPECIFICATIONS
FIG.	FIGURE	SQ FT	SQUARE FEET
FIN.	FINISH	SRWY	STAIRWAY
FL	FLOOR	ST	STEEL
FLASH.	FLASHING	STOR	STORAGE
F. O.	FINISH OPENING	STRUCT	STRUCTURAL
FS	FULL SIZE	SUSP	SUSPENDED
GA	GAUGE	T	TREAD, THICKNESS
GALV	GALVANIZED	THRESH	THRESHOLD
G I	GALVANIZED IRON	TYP	TYPICAL
GIWT	GLAZED INT WALL TILE	UNFIN	UNFINISHED
GL	GLASS	UR	URINAL
GYP BL	GYPSUM BLOCK	V	VINYL
HC	HOLLOW CORE	V.A.T.	VINYL ASBESTOS TILE
HDWE	HARDWARE	VERT.	VERTICAL
HM	HOLLOW METAL	VEST	VESTIBULE
HORIZ.	HORIZONTAL	V. T.	VINYL TILE
HT	HEIGHT	W	WAX, WIDTH
HW	HOT WATER	WC	WATER CLOSET
I. D.	INSIDE DIMENSION	WD	WOOD, WORKING DRAWINGS
INSUL	INSULATION	WDW	WINDOW
INT	INTERIOR	W I	WROUGHT IRON
K	KITCHEN	WP	WATERPROOF
KCP	KEENE'S CEMENT PLASTER		

| 21 | PROJECT ARCHITECTURAL DRAFTING STANDARDS AND SYMBOLS | MISCELLANEOUS PROJECT DRAFTING STANDARDS AND SYMBOLS | |

Formulate additional project drafting standards and symbols, if required. Devise them to complement standards and symbols shown in Chapters 16 through 20.

22 | **STANDARD FORMAT FOR ARCHITECTURAL WORKING DRAWINGS** | **TECHNIQUES FOR PRESENTING ARCHITECTURAL DRAWINGS** |

TECHNIQUES FOR PRESENTING ARCHITECTURAL DRAWINGS

Standard Techniques for Presenting Architectural Drawings are used to produce efficiently-prepared, unambiguous, unified drawings and to reduce confusion in the building industry. Like Office Architectural Drafting Standards and Symbols, Techniques for Presenting Architectural Drawings do not convey information directly; consequently, they are not shown and explained in sets of architectural working drawings but are printed and issued to draftsmen. See illustrations and descriptions of Techniques for Presenting Architectural Drawings in the five chapters listed below:

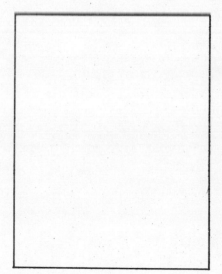

DRAWING PROCESS

See pages 126-127 for steps normally followed in preparation of architectural working drawings and pages 121-125 for drawing arrangements.

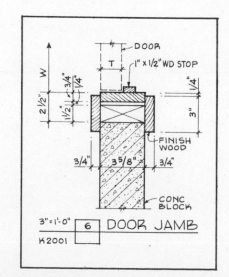

| 23 | TECHNIQUES FOR PRE-SENTING ARCHITECTURAL DRAWINGS | DIMENSIONS | |

GENERAL

Design and construction information is conveyed graphically in architectural working drawings with linework, including conventions and symbols, augmented by notes and dimensions. Dimensions size and locate buildings and site improvements on sites; and size and locate building components (masses), spaces, and built-in contents.

Dimensioning on drawings is composed of overall dimensions and particular dimensions. Overall dimensions are the largest height, width, and depth dimensions on drawings. Particular dimensions are smaller height, width, and depth dimensions that locate and/or size contents of drawings. A particular dimension on one drawing may be an overall dimension on another drawing. For example, on small scale sections through buildings, floor to ceiling dimensions are particular dimensions; on interior elevations, they are overall dimensions. Overall dimensions are normally placed outside drawings with dimension lines and dimension extension lines. Particular dimensions are placed outside or inside drawings with dimension lines, and dimension extension lines where required.

Dimension drawings (using the inch-foot system) with dimension lines, and dimension extension lines where required. Place dimensions above horizontal dimension lines, or where limited by space, below dimension lines. Place dimensions to the left of vertical dimension lines, or where limited by space, to the right of dimension lines. Face bottoms of dimensions at horizontal dimension lines toward bottoms of drawing sheets. Face bottoms of dimensions at vertical dimension lines toward right sides of drawing sheets. If dimensions cannot be placed properly between appropriate dimension extension lines and/or object or profile lines, place them outside the lines. Use note lines from dimensions to desired dimension areas at dimension lines, if required to clarify dimensioning.

Vertical dimensions consist of height dimensions only. Horizontal dimensions consist of both width (or breadth) and depth (or length) dimensions. Indicate vertical dimensions on small scale elevations and vertical sections, horizontal dimensions on small scale plans and horizontal sections, and vertical and/or horizontal

dimensions on large scale details as required to locate and size contents of details. Indicate height and width or height and depth dimensions on elevation and vertical section details and width and depth dimensions on plan and horizontal section details. In a series of interrelated multiview details, do not indicate width or depth dimensions on elevation and vertical section details unless necessary. For example, indicate height dimensions on window head and sill details and indicate width and depth dimensions on window jamb and vertical mullion details. Horizontal width and depth dimensions may be indicated on small scale elevations and vertical sections, and vertical height dimensions and elevations may be noted on small scale plans and horizontal sections, if the dimensions or elevations simplify drawings.

Horizontal width dimensions for built-in cabinetwork are normally indicated on interior elevations rather than on floor plans. Horizontal depth dimensions for built-in cabinetwork are indicated on floor plans or detail drawings or are noted on interior elevations.

Place dimensions near linework dimensioned inside or outside object or profile lines so that graphic and written information will not be obscured. Differentiate dimensioning on small scale drawings and on liberally dimensioned large scale detail drawings by placing dimensions in two or more parallel rows. Indicate largest dimensions at dimension lines farthest from object or profile lines and smallest dimensions at dimension lines nearest to object or profile lines. Place overall dimensions and selected particular dimensions on small scale general drawings. Do not place overall small scale drawing dimensions on large scale detail drawings. They would unnecessarily duplicate dimensions shown on small scale drawings and would particularize large scale detail drawings. A greater number of less applicable detail drawings would result.

Exterior elevations may have as many as four rows of vertical dimensions; namely, overall (usually from main floor level to top of roof or parapet), floor and roof levels, ceiling heights if required, and window (and door) openings. Small scale sections through buildings may have three rows of vertical dimensions; namely, overall, floor and roof levels, and ceiling heights. Interior elevations normally have at least two rows of vertical dimensions; namely, floor to ceiling and room features (such as wainscots, cabinetwork, and mirrors). Small scale floor plans may have as many as five rows of horizontal dimensions; namely, overall, column center line, exterior wall breaks, window and door openings, and exterior wall thicknesses.

Correlate dimensioning (and use the elevation mark symbol) to better relate large scale detail drawings to small scale drawings. Include key dimensions on large scale detail drawings in dimensioning on small scale drawings. For example, if a 2″ height dimension is indicated for a horizontal curtain wall mullion on a large scale detail drawing, include the key 2″ dimension in the string of vertical curtain wall dimensions on small scale elevations. Where practical, use dimension extension lines as dimension reference lines by adding suffixes to dimensions on small scale drawings, such as W and HT, and indicating suffixes only for dimensions on related large scale detail drawings.

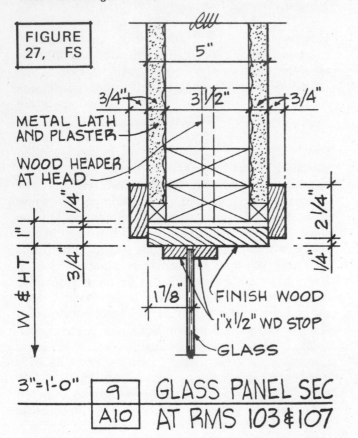

FIGURE 27, FS

METAL LATH AND PLASTER

WOOD HEADER AT HEAD

FINISH WOOD

1″x½″ WD STOP

GLASS

3″=1′-0″   9 / A10   GLASS PANEL SEC AT RMS 103 & 107

To control redundancy in a set of architectural working drawings, dimensioning of some building components shown in small scale general drawings and in some small scale detail drawings must be closely coordinated. Scales and contents of these drawings are discussed in Chapter 11. Dimensioning of these drawings is discussed in this chapter. Examples of dimensions, notes, and

titles for drawings in architectural working drawings are shown in this chapter and in Chapter 24.

SITE PLAN DIMENSIONS

Locate new buildings horizontally on site plans with dimension lines from building perimeter lines to property lines, or, if necessary, to other significant lines, such as existing building lines. Indicate widths and depths of new buildings with dimension lines. Position new buildings vertically by finish ground floor or finish first floor elevations indicated within building perimeter lines. Indicate finish grades at building corners by spot elevations.

Indicate vertical locations of sewer lines by invert elevations at critical points on sewer lines if necessary. Indicate vertical locations of water mains, telephone lines, power lines, and gas mains by notes on site plans or in specifications if satisfactory. Indicate horizontal locations of service extensions of public utilities by dimensions if necessary. Locate and size site improvements horizontally on site plans with dimension lines, and note critical elevations.

Detailed explanations of site plan dimensions, spot elevations, and contour lines are contained in the book *The Site Plan in Architectural Working Drawings* by George T. Clayton, published by Stipes Publishing Company, Champaign, Illinois 61820.

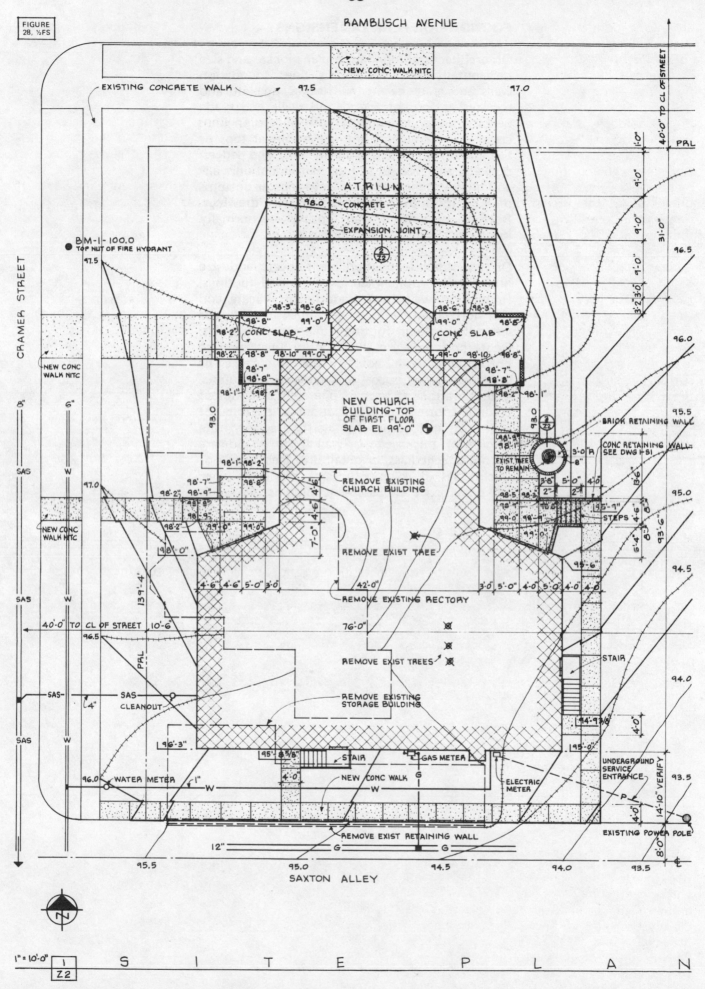

FIGURE 28, ½FS

RAMBUSCH AVENUE

SITE PLAN

1" = 10'-0"

FOUNDATION PLAN DIMENSIONS

On architectural foundation plans locate and size horizontally with dimension lines foundation walls and grade beams, and ledges, pockets, and recesses at tops of foundation walls and grade beams; locate horizontally with dimension lines crawl space columns; note elevations at tops of foundation walls and grade beams, and ledges, pockets, and recesses at tops of foundation walls and grade beams; and note elevations at bottoms of wall footings if required to clarify drawings. Bottoms of exterior wall footings are normally located vertically on exterior elevations.

On structural foundation plans locate and size horizontally with dimension lines wall footings, foundation walls, and grade beams; locate and size horizontally with notes, dimension lines, or schedules column footings, pile caps, and piles; locate horizontally with dimension lines and size horizontally with notes, dimension lines, or schedules crawl space and basement columns; note elevations at tops of pile caps and tops of column footings; note elevations at bottoms of wall footings if required to clarify drawings; note heights or thicknesses of wall footings; indicate by notes, schedules, or detail drawings heights or thicknesses of column footings, pile caps, piles, and crawl space and basement columns.

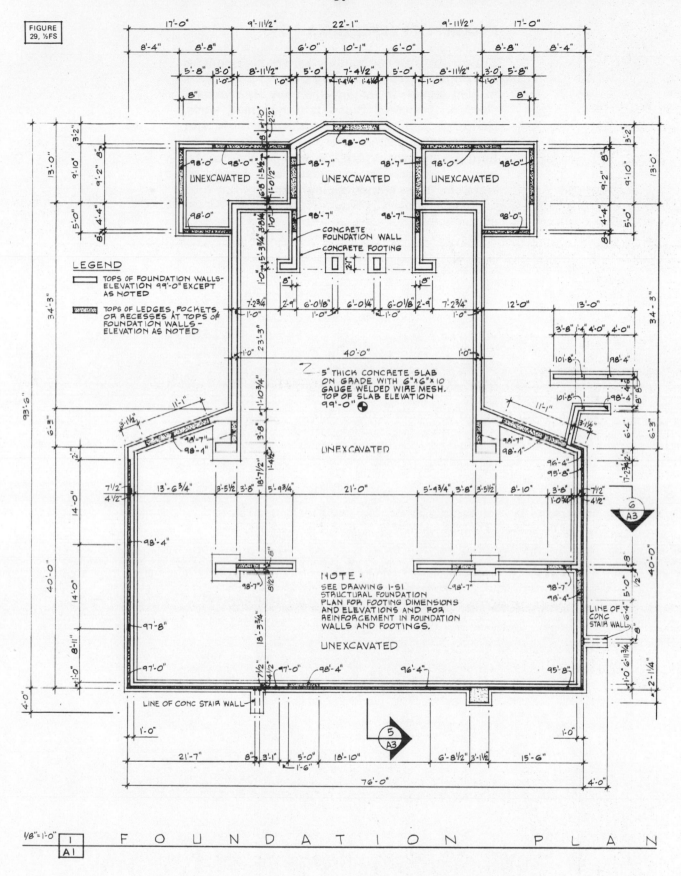

FIGURE 29, ½FS

LEGEND

☐ TOPS OF FOUNDATION WALLS-
ELEVATION 99'-0" EXCEPT
AS NOTED

▨ TOPS OF LEDGES, POCKETS,
OR RECESSES AT TOPS OF
FOUNDATION WALLS-
ELEVATION AS NOTED

UNEXCAVATED

UNEXCAVATED

UNEXCAVATED

CONCRETE
FOUNDATION WALL

CONCRETE FOOTING

5" THICK CONCRETE SLAB
ON GRADE WITH 6"×6"×10
GAUGE WELDED WIRE MESH.
TOP OF SLAB ELEVATION
99'-0"

UNEXCAVATED

NOTE:
SEE DRAWING 1-S1
STRUCTURAL FOUNDATION
PLAN FOR FOOTING DIMENSIONS
AND ELEVATIONS AND FOR
REINFORCEMENT IN FOUNDATION
WALLS AND FOOTINGS.

UNEXCAVATED

LINE OF CONC STAIR WALL

LINE OF
CONC
STAIR WALL

1/8"=1'-0" 1
A1   FOUNDATION PLAN

FLOOR PLAN DIMENSIONS

Locate and size horizontally with dimension lines such building components shown on floor plans in plan section as columns (columns are normally sized on structural drawings only), piers, walls, partitions, and wall and partition openings, and such building components shown in plan view as built-in cabinetwork, stairs, ramps, hatches, access panels, elevators, dumbwaiters, and escalators. Note elevations at tops of floor drains.

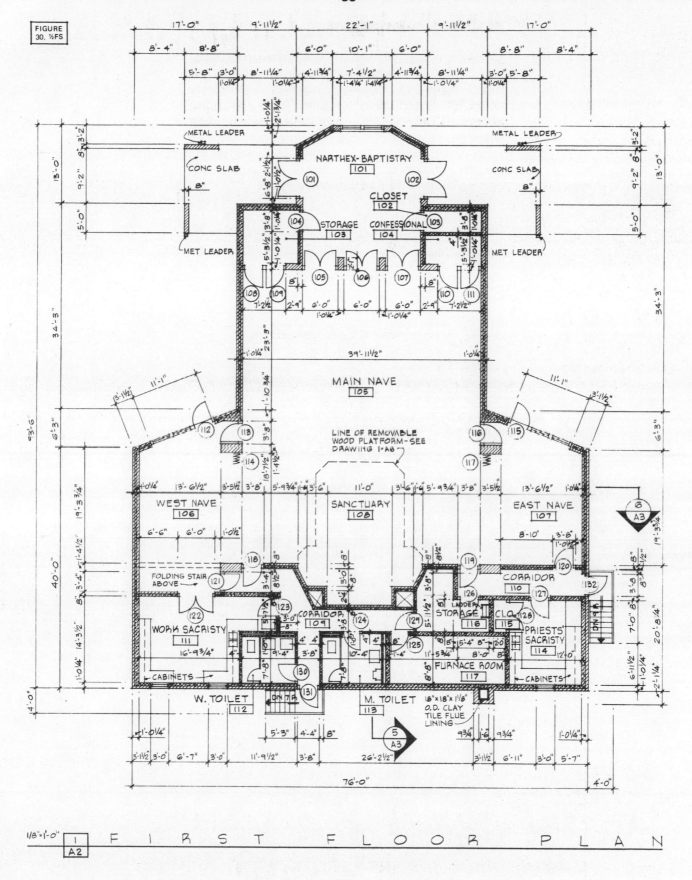

FIGURE 30, ½FS

NARTHEX-BAPTISTRY
101

CLOSET
102

STORAGE
103

CONFESSIONAL
104

MAIN NAVE
105

LINE OF REMOVABLE
WOOD PLATFORM-SEE
DRAWING 1-A8

WEST NAVE
106

SANCTUARY
108

EAST NAVE
107

CORRIDOR
110

FOLDING STAIR
ABOVE

WORK SACRISTY
111

CORRIDOR
109

STORAGE
116

CLO
115

PRIESTS'
SACRISTY
114

CABINETS

FURNACE ROOM
117

CABINETS

W. TOILET
112

M. TOILET
113

18"x18"x1⅛"
O.D. CLAY
TILE FLUE
LINING

METAL LEADER

CONC SLAB

MET LEADER

METAL LEADER

CONC SLAB

MET LEADER

LADDER

ROOF PLAN DIMENSIONS

Locate and size horizontally with dimension lines, if required, such building components shown on roof plans as copings, scuttles, skylights, chimneys, gutters, and scuppers. Note elevations at tops of roof drains. Indicate roof elevations as required.

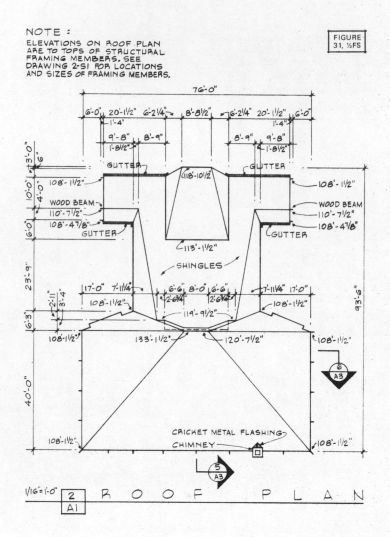

NOTE :
ELEVATIONS ON ROOF PLAN
ARE TO TOPS OF STRUCTURAL
FRAMING MEMBERS. SEE
DRAWING 2-51 FOR LOCATIONS
AND SIZES OF FRAMING MEMBERS.

FIGURE
31, ½FS

EXTERIOR ELEVATION DIMENSIONS

Locate and size vertically with dimension lines such building components shown on exterior elevations as wall footings, foundation walls, exterior walls, steps, doors (if necessary), windows (window heights if necessary), roofs, skylights, and chimneys. Do not relate vertical dimensions to grade lines at building shown on exterior elevations, or use grade lines as dimension reference lines, since they may not be accurately located. Exact locations of grade lines are indicated by contour lines and/or spot elevations on site plans.

Locate levels of major horizontal building components on exterior elevations with dimension lines and dimension extension lines placed outside elevations. Levels include bottoms of wall footings, tops of floors and roofs, bottoms of suspended ceilings if necessary, and bottoms of window (and door) lintels if necessary. Place the elevation mark symbol on floor level and roof level dimension extension lines. In the same area, note floor and roof levels, materials or surfaces, and elevations. For example, say, "First floor concrete slab elevation 106'-8'," or "Second floor finish floor elevation 119'-4'." Dimension roof levels to tops of structural roof slabs or decks, or to tops of structural framing members if more practical. Dimension floor levels to tops of finish floors or to tops of structural floor slabs or decks where finish floors are thin flooring materials less than 7/8" in total thickness, such as resilient flooring and carpeting.

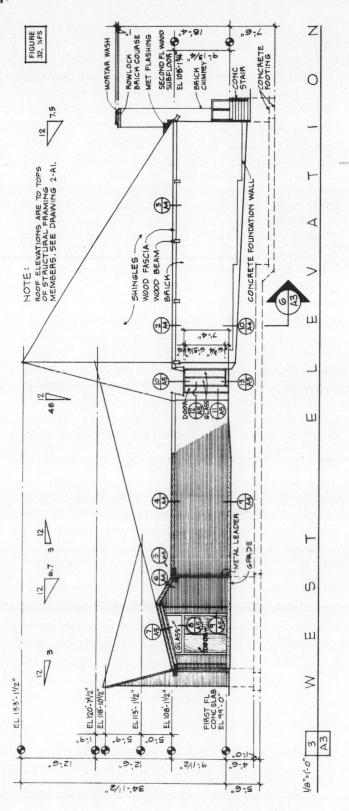

SMALL SCALE SECTION THROUGH BUILDING DIMENSIONS

Locate and size vertically with dimension lines such building components shown on small scale sections through building as floors and roofs. Locate and/or size vertically with dimension lines such building elements, features, and variations shown in section as large wall openings (except doors and windows), wall projections, and changes in suspended ceiling heights. For sections that scale 1/4" = 1'-0" and over, locate and/or size vertically with dimension lines such building features shown in elevation as large wall openings (except doors and windows referenced and detailed from door reference symbol and window reference symbol), nonceiling high partitions, wainscots, cabinetwork, shelves, mirrors, chalkboards, tackboards, and borrowed lights.

Locate levels of major horizontal building components on small scale sections through building with dimension lines and dimension extension lines placed outside sections. Levels include tops of floors and roofs and bottoms of suspended ceilings. Place the elevation mark symbol on floor level and roof level dimension extension lines. In the same area, note floor and roof levels, materials or surfaces, and elevations. Dimension and note floor and roof levels identical to floor and roof dimensioning and noting indicated on exterior elevations.

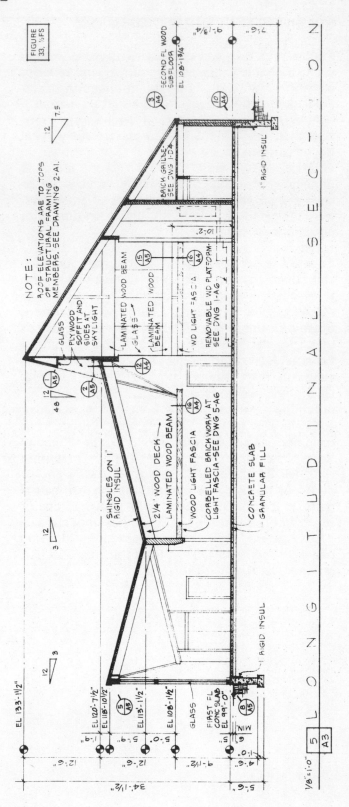

STAIR SECTION DIMENSIONS

Contrary to the general rule of indicating vertical height dimensions only on small scale elevations and vertical sections, indicate horizontal width or depth dimensions on small scale vertical longitudinal sections through stairs and on stair elevations to better relate runs to flights and treads to risers. On longitudinal stair sections and on stair elevations locate and size vertically stair flights, floors, stair landings, and stair risers; and locate and size horizontally stair runs, stair landings, and stair treads with dimension lines and dimension extension lines.

Dimension stair landing depths, stair tread widths, and stair runs from finish faces of risers (not from faces of nosings). On longitudinal stair sections and on stair elevations indicate number of treads, width of individual treads, and aggregate width of treads for each stair run with dimension lines and dimension extension lines. For example, on a stair section, a stair run dimension indication from the

face of a stair riser to the face of a landing riser may indicate "9 treads @ 10½"=7'-10½"."

On longitudinal stair sections and on stair elevations dimension stairs vertically with two strings of dimensions for stairs with landings and one string of dimensions for stairs without landings, using dimension lines and dimension extension lines. In all strings of dimensions, indicate number of risers, height of individual risers to the nearest 1/16", and aggregate height of risers (equal to distance between levels dimensioned). For example, on a stair section, a stair flight dimension indication from a floor to a stair landing may indicate "10 risers @ 7 3/16"+=6'-0"." Dimension floor and stair landing levels in the same manner as floor and roof dimensioning indicated in exterior elevations and small scale sections through building. Place the elevation mark symbol on dimension extension lines at floor and roof levels only. In the same area, note floor and roof levels, materials or surfaces, and elevations if required.

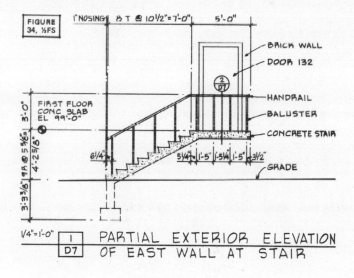

PARTIAL EXTERIOR ELEVATION
OF EAST WALL AT STAIR

INTERIOR ELEVATION DIMENSIONS

Locate and/or size vertically with dimension lines such building elements and features shown on interior elevations as large wall openings (except doors and windows referenced and detailed from door reference symbol and window reference symbol), nonceiling high partitions, wainscots, cabinetwork, shelves, mirrors, chalkboards, tackboards, and borrowed lights.

Indicate floor to ceiling dimensions, with dimension lines and dimension extension lines placed outside elevations, from tops of finish floors or from tops of structural floor slabs or decks where finish floors are thin flooring materials less than 7/8'' in total thickness to bottoms of finish ceilings.

Horizontal width and depth dimensions may be indicated on interior elevations if the dimensions simplify drawings. Add the word "verify" after overall horizontal dimensions, since horizontal dimensions on plans normally take precedence over redundant horizontal dimensions on interior elevations, exterior elevations, and small scale sections through building.

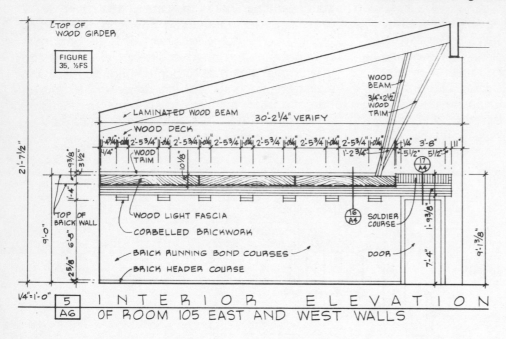

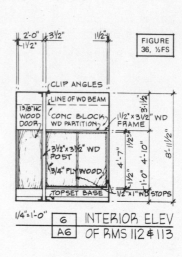

DETAIL PLAN DIMENSIONS

Locate and size horizontally with dimension lines building components and features shown on detail floor plans, finish flooring plans, and reflected ceiling plans. Indicate particular dimensions on detail plans as required to explain drawings. Indicate overall dimensions on detail plans where practical to better coordinate detail plans with small scale floor plans. If particular or overall dimensions on detail plans are to finish surfaces and are different from dimensions indicated on small scale floor plans, indicate names of finish surfaces and dimensions from finish surfaces to rough surfaces on detail plans so that dimensions on detail plans correspond to dimensions on small scale floor plans. Indicate overall room dimensions only on portions of small scale floor plans that are augmented by detail floor plans.

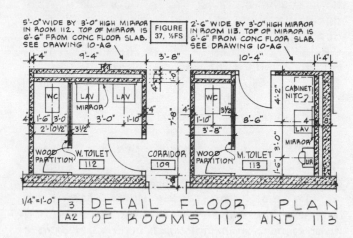

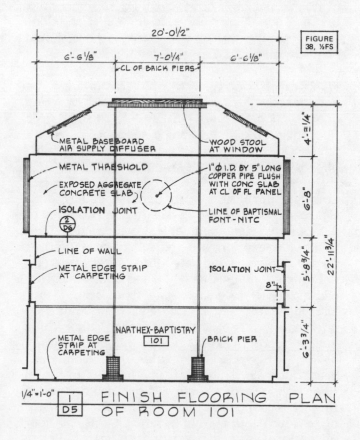

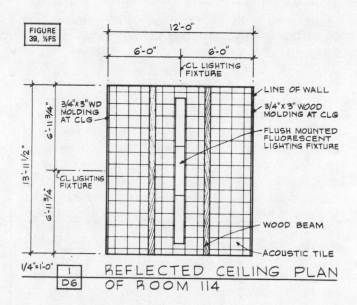

DOOR DIMENSIONING

To facilitate door fabrication, door frame construction, and door frame installation, use two sets of dimensions for door heights and door widths in architectural working drawings; namely, door dimensions and door rough opening dimensions. Door dimensions relate to door fabrication and door operations and are smaller than door rough opening dimensions that relate to door frame construction and door frame installations.

Door dimension heights are usually measured from finish door (frame) heads to tops of finish floors or to tops of structural floor slabs or decks, if finish flooring is less than 7/8" in total thickness. Door dimension heights for doors with bottom frames (not thresholds), such as (side) sliding doors, are usually measured from finish door (frame) heads to finish door frame sills. Door dimension widths are usually measured from finish door (frame) jambs to finish door (frame) jambs.

Door rough opening dimension heights are usually measured from bottoms of lintels to tops of finish floors or to tops of structural floor slabs or decks, if finish flooring is less than 7/8" in total thickness. Door rough opening dimension heights, for doors with bottom door frames, are usually measured from bottoms of lintels to tops of subfloors or blocking. Door rough opening dimension widths are usually measured from faces of lintel supports or blocking to faces of lintel supports or blocking. Door thicknesses are measured from finish door surface to finish door surface.

Indicate door dimensions to door dimension reference lines, and indicate door rough opening dimensions to door rough opening dimension reference lines. These reference lines are normally dimension extension lines in architectural working drawings. Show door dimension heights and widths on elevations of door types in the direct reference method of door referencing and in door schedules in the schedule method of door referencing. Show door rough opening dimension widths on small scale floor plans, if necessary to clarify drawings. Show door rough opening dimension heights on exterior elevations and interior elevations, if necessary to clarify drawings. Show door dimension reference lines and door rough opening dimension reference lines on door frame details and indicate dimension between reference lines on each door frame detail drawing.

Locate exterior doors horizontally on small scale floor plans with dimension lines, placed outside plans, from building corners and adjacent wall openings to door jamb rough opening dimension reference lines, normally faces of lintel supports or blocking. Dimension exterior door rough opening widths on small scale floor plans from door jamb rough opening dimension reference lines to door jamb rough opening dimension reference lines. Horizontal locations of interior doors may be determined by scaling drawings. If greater accuracy is required, locate interior doors horizontally on small scale floor plans with dimension lines to door jamb rough opening dimension reference lines. If required to explain design or construction, dimension interior door rough opening widths on small scale floor plans from door jamb rough opening dimension reference lines to door jamb rough opening dimension reference lines.

Do not indicate door rough opening dimension heights on exterior elevations or on interior elevations, unless dimensions are required to explain design or construction. Door rough opening dimension heights are obtained by adding door dimension heights, indicated on elevations of door types or in door schedules, to dimensions between door dimension reference lines and door rough opening dimension reference lines shown on door head (and door sill) detail drawings.

When exact door types or door frames are to be determined after completion of working drawings, locate doors horizontally on small scale floor plans by dimensioning to doorway center lines. Do not indicate door rough opening dimension heights on elevations.

Correlate dimensioning in door schedules, door types, and door frame details by dimensioning to appropriate reference lines and by adding suffixes to door dimensions. In the schedule method of door referencing indicate door thicknesses (T), door dimension heights (HT), and door dimension widths (W) in appropriate spaces in Door Schedules. In the direct reference method of door referencing on elevation of each door type indicate door thickness by note; door dimension height, suffixed by the letters HT, from door head dimension reference line to top of finish floor or to top of structural floor slab or deck, if finish flooring is less than 7/8" in total thickness, or to door sill dimension reference line; and door dimension width, suffixed by the letter W, from door jamb dimension reference line to door jamb dimension reference line. On each door jamb detail, indicate T for door thickness. On each door head detail, indicate HT for door dimension height from door head dimension reference line; on each door jamb detail (and each door vertical mullion detail), indicate W for door dimension width from door jamb dimension reference line; and on each door sill detail, indicate HT for door dimension height from door sill dimension reference line.

DOOR REFERENCE LINES NTS

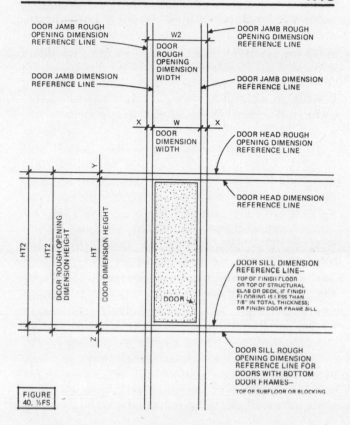

DOOR JAMB ROUGH OPENING DIMENSION REFERENCE LINE

DOOR JAMB ROUGH OPENING DIMENSION REFERENCE LINE

W2

DOOR ROUGH OPENING DIMENSION WIDTH

DOOR JAMB DIMENSION REFERENCE LINE

DOOR JAMB DIMENSION REFERENCE LINE

X W X

DOOR DIMENSION WIDTH

DOOR HEAD ROUGH OPENING DIMENSION REFERENCE LINE

DOOR HEAD DIMENSION REFERENCE LINE

HT2

HT2

DOOR ROUGH OPENING DIMENSION HEIGHT

HT

DOOR DIMENSION HEIGHT

DOOR

DOOR SILL DIMENSION REFERENCE LINE— TOP OF FINISH FLOOR OR TOP OF STRUCTURAL SLAB OR DECK, IF FINISH FLOORING IS LESS THAN 7/8" IN TOTAL THICKNESS; OR FINISH DOOR FRAME SILL

DOOR SILL ROUGH OPENING DIMENSION REFERENCE LINE FOR DOORS WITH BOTTOM DOOR FRAMES— TOP OF SUBFLOOR OR BLOCKING

FIGURE 40, ½FS

NOTE:
X, Y, AND Z DIMENSIONS ARE INDICATED ON DOOR FRAME DETAIL DRAWINGS.
W AND HT DIMENSIONS ARE INDICATED ON DOOR TYPES OR IN DOOR SCHEDULES.
W2 DIMENSIONS ARE INDICATED ON SMALL SCALE FLOOR PLANS, IF NECESSARY.
HT2 DIMENSIONS ARE INDICATED ON EXTERIOR AND INTERIOR ELEVATIONS, IF NECESSARY.

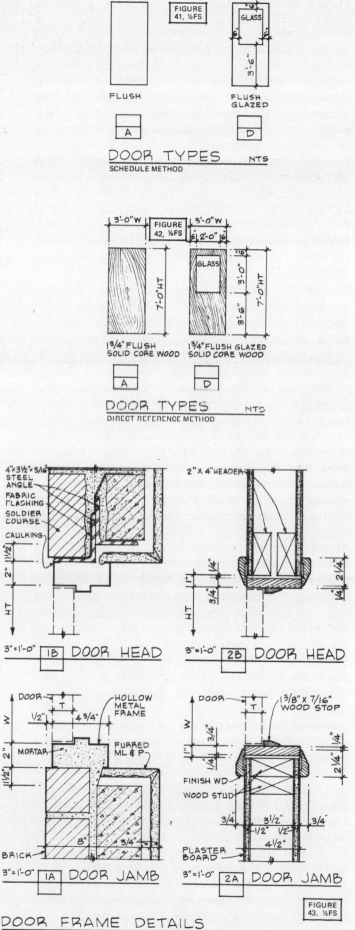

FIGURE 41, ½FS

FLUSH

FLUSH GLAZED

GLASS

3'-6"

A

D

DOOR TYPES NTS
SCHEDULE METHOD

FIGURE 42, ½FS

3'-0" W

3'-0" W

2'-0"

7'-0" HT

7'-0" HT

GLASS

3'-0"

3'-6"

1¾" FLUSH SOLID CORE WOOD

1¾" FLUSH GLAZED SOLID CORE WOOD

A

D

DOOR TYPES NTS
DIRECT REFERENCE METHOD

4"x3½"x5/16" STEEL ANGLE
FABRIC FLASHING
SOLDIER COURSE
CAULKING

2" X 4" HEADER

2" 11½"

HT

3" = 1'-0" 1B DOOR HEAD

1"

¾"

2¼"

HT

3" = 1'-0" 2B DOOR HEAD

DOOR

T

½"

4¾"

W

MORTAR

2"

1½"

HOLLOW METAL FRAME

FURRED ML & P

BRICK

8"

¾"

3" = 1'-0" 1A DOOR JAMB

DOOR

T

W

¾"

HT

1¾"

2¼"

1⅜" X 7/16" WOOD STOP

FINISH WD
WOOD STUD

PLASTER BOARD

¾"

3½"

¾"

½" ½"

4½"

3" = 1'-0" 2A DOOR JAMB

FIGURE 43, ½FS

DOOR FRAME DETAILS
SCHEDULE METHOD   JAMBS ONLY ARE SHOWN IN DIRECT REFERENCE METHOD

WINDOW AND CURTAIN WALL DIMENSIONING

To facilitate window fabrication and installation, use two sets of dimensions for window heights and window widths in architectural working drawings; namely, window dimensions and window rough opening dimensions. For mass produced conventional windows these dimensions are invariably assigned by window manufacturers. Window dimensions relate to window fabrication and sash operations and are smaller than window rough opening dimensions that relate to window installations.

Window dimension heights and widths are usually measured to or near window frame outer edges. Window rough opening dimension heights and widths are usually measured to or near building surfaces, such as bottoms of lintels, faces of lintel supports or blocking, tops of rough walls or blocking, or to faces of curtain wall horizontal and vertical mullions.

Indicate window dimensions to window dimension reference lines, and indicate window rough opening dimensions to window rough opening dimension reference lines. These reference lines are normally dimension extension lines in architectural working drawings. Show window dimension heights and widths on elevations of window types. Show window rough opening dimension widths on small scale floor plans. Show window rough opening dimension heights on exterior elevations, if necessary to clarify drawings. Show window dimension reference lines and window rough opening dimension reference lines on window details and indicate dimension between reference lines on each window detail drawing.

Locate and size windows on small scale floor plans and exterior elevations (size if required) with dimension lines and dimension extension lines placed outside drawings where possible. Locate windows vertically on exterior elevations from floor lines to window head rough opening dimension reference lines. If necessary to clarify drawings, indicate window rough opening dimension heights on exterior elevations from window head rough opening dimension reference lines to window sill rough opening dimension reference lines. Locate windows horizontally on small scale floor plans from building corners and adjacent wall openings to window jamb rough opening dimension reference lines. Indicate total window rough opening dimension widths, including window vertical mullion widths, on small scale floor plans from one window jamb rough opening dimension reference line to the opposite window jamb rough opening dimension reference line. If necessary to clarify drawings, indicate individual window rough opening dimension widths and individual window vertical mullion widths on small scale floor plans.

When window manufacturer or exact window types are to be determined after completion of working drawings, locate windows horizontally on small scale floor plans by dimensioning to window center lines, and locate windows vertically on exterior elevations by dimensioning to estimated window head rough opening dimension reference lines. Note "verify" after estimated vertical location dimensions.

Correlate dimensioning on window details and window types by dimensioning to appropriate reference lines and by adding suffixes to window dimensions. On elevation of each window type indicate window frame depth or thickness by note; window dimension height, suffixed by the letters HT, from window head dimension reference line to window sill dimension reference line; and window dimension width, suffixed by the letter W, from window jamb dimension reference line to window jamb dimension reference line. On each window jamb detail indicate window frame depth or thickness. On each window head detail (and each window horizontal mullion head detail), indicate HT for window dimension height from window head dimension reference line; on each window jamb detail (and each window vertical mullion detail), indicate W for window dimension width from window jamb dimension reference line; and on each window sill detail (and each horizontal mullion sill detail), indicate HT for window dimension height from window sill dimension reference line.

Dimension curtain walls horizontally on small scale floor plans and vertically on exterior elevations with dimension lines placed outside plans and outside elevations where practical. Indicate panel widths, mullion widths, and spacing between vertical mullions on small scale floor plans; and horizontal mullion heights, spacings between horizontal mullions, and operating sash and fixed panel heights on exterior elevations. Tie strings of vertical curtain wall dimensions to each floor line. Dimension curtain wall window rough opening dimension widths on small scale floor plans and window rough opening dimension heights on exterior elevations to appropriate window head, horizontal mullion, sill, jamb, and vertical mullion rough opening dimension reference lines. These reference lines are normally dimension extension lines to faces of mullions and panels.

Correlate curtain wall window dimensioning on curtain wall details, small scale floor plans, and exterior elevations with key (mullion width) dimensions. Indicate vertical and horizontal mullion widths on curtain wall detail drawings, small scale floor plans, and exterior elevations.

WINDOW REFERENCE LINES   NTS

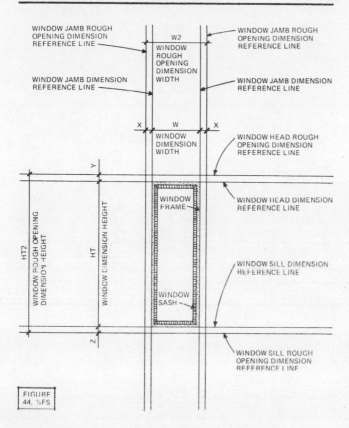

FIGURE 44, ½FS

NOTE:
X, Y, AND Z DIMENSIONS ARE INDICATED ON WINDOW DETAIL DRAWING.
W AND HT DIMENSIONS ARE INDICATED ON WINDOW TYPES.
W2 DIMENSIONS ARE INDICATED ON SMALL SCALE FLOOR PLANS.
HT2 DIMENSIONS ARE INDICATED ON EXTERIOR ELEVATIONS, IF NECESSARY.

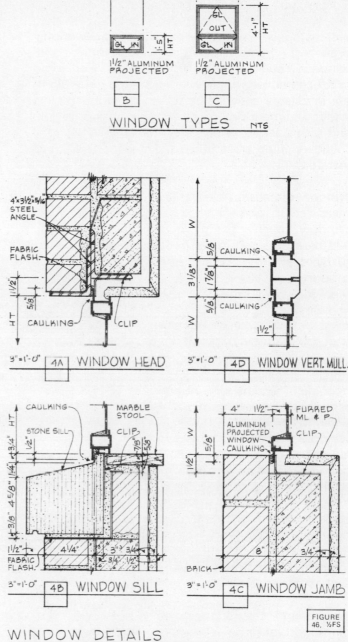

WINDOW TYPES   NTS

WINDOW DETAILS

FIGURE 46, ½FS

| 24 | TECHNIQUES FOR PRE-SENTING ARCHITECTURAL DRAWINGS | NOTES, AND TITLES FOR DRAWINGS | |

GENERAL

Design and construction information is conveyed graphically in architectural working drawings with linework, including conventions and symbols, augmented by notes and dimensions. Notes identify individual lines and clarify or explain graphic information contained in related linework. Titles for drawings describe drawings and locate details on building sites or in buildings. Examples of dimensions, notes, and titles for drawings in architectural working drawings are shown in this chapter and in Chapter 23.

NOTES

Most required written information on drawings can be stated in one word, a few words, or in a phrase. Complete sentences are rarely required. Make notes brief and descriptive rather than lengthy and directive. Use descriptive notes (not directive notes) to identify individual lines or to clarify information contained in related linework. For example, say "caulking" (not "caulk") to identify caulking in window jamb details. If required to make drawings understandable, use directive notes to explain mechanical operations or construction processes inferred in drawings or to refer readers to specifications or other drawings. If directive notes are lengthy, place them near relevant drawings under headings titled "Notes." Where spaces for notes are limited, abbreviate words. Use standard abbreviations in notes and include abbreviations in List of Abbreviations.

Descriptive notes may identify materials and/or indicate building components, elements, or features. For example, a note may read, "stone," "stone coping," or "coping." Include names of building components, elements, or features in notes on drawings where necessary to clarify drawings and where necessary to better coordinate specifications with drawings. For example, if the words "wood edge strip" are used in a roofing specification, identify the strip on drawings by note using the same terminology; namely, "wood edge strip."

Add purpose or use information to descriptive notes that identify materials, if necessary to make work shown on drawings more understandable. For example, "mortar setting bed" may be said rather than "mortar." Do not use purpose or use information alone as notes. Do not say, "setting bed."

Identify material indications in elevation on drawings by notes. If necessary to clarify drawings, identify material indications in section on drawings by notes. Identify structural, mechanical, and electrical items or equipment by descriptive notes. Do not indicate sizes in these notes, since sizes are indicated in structural, mechanical, or electrical drawings or specifications. For example, say, "concrete beam," not "14" x 22" concrete beam." Do not describe quality of materials or finishes or standards of workmanship by notes on (original) drawings. This information would unnecessarily duplicate information in specifications. Furthermore, it would particularize large scale detail drawings and would result in a greater number of less applicable detail drawings.

To reduce production costs and number of drawings, use generic names in notes on drawings where practical, specific names in schedules, and specific and proprietary names in specifications. For example, say, "resilient flooring" in notes on drawings, "vinyl tile" in room finish schedules, and "vinyl tile" and "marbeldeck" in specifications. This procedure permits minor changes to be made in proposed building design and construction after completion of working drawings and specifications by issuing inexpensive addenda to specifications, and to schedules if necessary, without making expensive (and often confusing) revisions to drawings. This procedure also generalizes large scale detail drawings, resulting in a lesser number of more applicable detail drawings. Other examples of generic names for specific names used in notes on architectural working drawings are "metal" for copper, "granular fill" for gravel, and "built-up roofing" for four ply tar and gravel roofing.

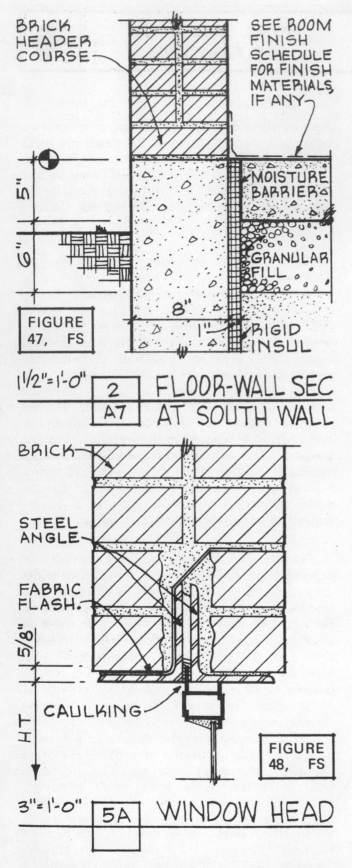

BRICK
HEADER
COURSE

SEE ROOM
FINISH
SCHEDULE
FOR FINISH
MATERIALS,
IF ANY

5"

6"

MOISTURE
BARRIER

GRANULAR
FILL

FIGURE
47, FS

8"

1"

RIGID
INSUL.

1 1/2"=1'-0" | 2 / A7 | FLOOR-WALL SEC AT SOUTH WALL

BRICK

STEEL
ANGLE

FABRIC
FLASH.

5/8"

HT

CAULKING

FIGURE
48, FS

3"=1'-0" | 5A | WINDOW HEAD

Use specific names on drawings to identify items that are not substitutable. For example, on a window head detail drawing that shows steel angles, note the angles as "steel angles," not as "metal angles." Use specific names on drawings to confirm identity of items substantially identified by linework configurations. For example, on a

window jamb detail drawing that shows an extruded aluminum frame and projected extruded aluminum sash, note the window as "aluminum projected window," not as "metal projected window."

Place notes near explained linework inside or outside drawings in areas where they will not obscure graphic information. Where practical, group notes together in vertical alignment to facilitate comprehension of both graphic and written information. In large scale section detail drawings, place notes outside of section profile lines where possible to permit changes or additions to notes without affecting linework. Place notes judiciously so that note lines, from notes to explained linework, do not intersect.

Few, if any, building components or units are shown more extensively in a set of architectural working drawings than doors and windows. They are indicated in plans and elevations and explained by detail drawings. Notes on drawings concerning each of these two building units must be controlled to prevent unnecessary duplication of information and to coordinate drawings.

DOOR NOTES

In the schedule method of door referencing, describe doors with notes at elevations of door types. Under elevation of each door type note door style, such as "flush glazed." Note "glass" in elevations of door types with glass panels. Indicate types of glass, such as "1/4" float glass," in Door Schedules under Remarks column or in specifications. Complete door schedules for other necessary door information.

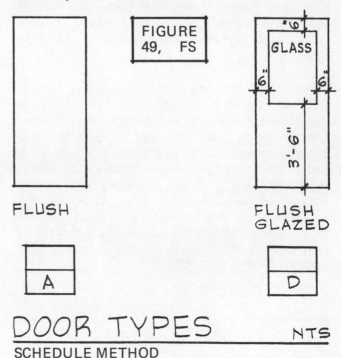

FLUSH

FLUSH
GLAZED

DOOR TYPES   NTS
SCHEDULE METHOD

In the direct reference method of door referencing, describe doors and indicate door thicknesses with notes at elevations of door types. Under elevation of each door type, note door thickness, door style, door construction, and door material, such as "1 3/4" flush glazed solid core wood." Note "glass" in elevations of door types with glass panels, if types and locations of glass are indicated in specifications. Note types of glass, such as "1/4" float glass," in elevations of door types with glass panels, if locations of glass are not included in specifications.

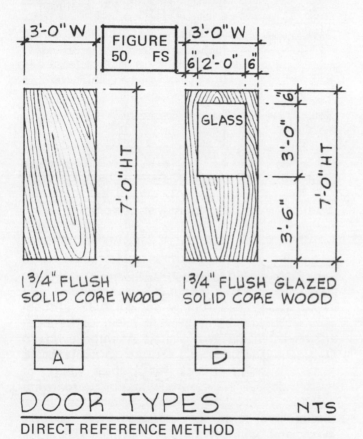

1¾" FLUSH SOLID CORE WOOD

1¾" FLUSH GLAZED SOLID CORE WOOD

DOOR TYPES NTS
DIRECT REFERENCE METHOD

Do not identify doors by notes in floor plans. Identify doors by notes in exterior elevations, interior elevations, and detail elevations, if required to clarify drawings.

WINDOW AND CURTAIN WALL NOTES

Describe windows and indicate window frame depths with notes at elevations of window types. Under elevation of each window type, note window frame depth or thickness, window frame material, and window type, such as "1 1/2" aluminum projected." If windows have operating sashes, indicate sash operations graphically. Note "glass" in elevations of window types, if types and locations of glass are indicated in specifications or on exterior elevations. Note types of glass, such as "1/4" float glass," in elevations of window types, if locations of glass

are not included in specifications or on exterior elevations. Do not identify (punched opening) windows by notes in floor plans or exterior elevations.

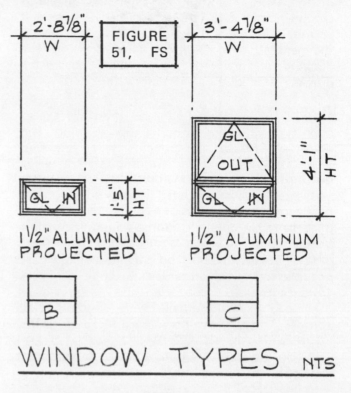

1½" ALUMINUM PROJECTED

1½" ALUMINUM PROJECTED

WINDOW TYPES NTS

Do not identify curtain wall windows by notes in small scale floor plans or exterior elevations. Although window reference symbols are not shown in curtain wall window operating sashes on exterior elevations as they are in punched opening windows, these sashes are identified graphically on exterior elevations by sash operating indications. Do not identify curtain walls by notes in floor plans. Identify curtain walls by notes in exterior elevations with such notes as "metal curtain wall," "glass," and "metal panel."

TITLES FOR DRAWINGS

Small scale detail drawings are referenced normally from small scale general drawings and schedules. Large scale detail drawings are referenced normally from small scale general drawings, small scale detail drawings, and schedules, and occasionally from related large scale detail drawings. The drawing reference symbol, denoting drawing number and sheet number on which drawing is presented, is shown on drawings at items detailed except at most doors and all (punched opening) windows. The title reference symbol, denoting drawing number and sheet number on which drawing is presented, is shown under all drawings except door types, door frame details, window types, and window details. The number reference system used with drawing reference symbol and title reference symbol identifies each drawing numerically and permits the reader to go from the general to the particular; to go from an item shown on small scale (or large scale) drawings to a detail drawing of the item. The number reference system is complemented by a title reference system that permits the reader to go from the particular to the general; to go from a detail drawing to a drawing or drawings from which the detail drawing is directly or indirectly referenced.

Place drawing titles under all drawings except door type drawings, window type drawings, and other building component type drawings referenced like door and window detail drawings. Titles should describe small scale general drawings and should describe detail drawings and locate details on building sites or in buildings. Locations of large scale details of some common building components; namely, entrance details, storefront details, window details, and door frame details are not required in drawing titles.

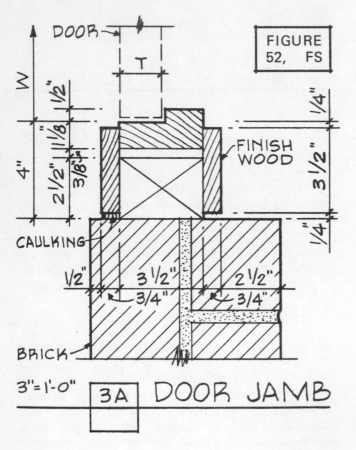

Descriptions of drawings in titles normally include identification of major building components shown in drawings or identification of significant drawing contents and identification of drawing form, such as "Foundation Plan," "North Exterior Elevation," "Section Through Building," and "Floor-Wall Section." Locations

of details in titles normally include specific or general locations of details on building sites or in buildings, such as "Section Through Retaining Wall--At Terrace," "Roof-Wall Section--At South Wall," "Floor-Wall Section--At Third Floor West Wall Between Column Lines 8 and 9," "Interior Elevation--Of Room 208," "Interior Elevation--Of Room 307 West Wall," and "Coping Section--Typical."

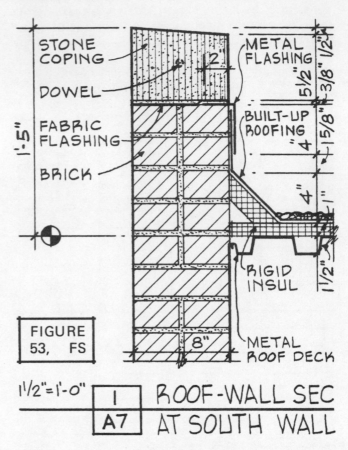

Group door type, door frame detail, window type, and window detail drawings separately. Place title reference symbol, denoting type letter or detail drawing number, under each drawing. Under each group of drawings on large-size working drawing sheets or in title blocks on small-size detail sheets, place group drawing title: "Door Types," "Door Frame Details," "Window Types," or "Window Details."

Place group drawing title, without title reference symbol, under each group of related large scale detail drawings, such as "Curtain Wall Details," "Threshold Details," and "Base Details." For building construction detail drawings referenced from small scale sections through buildings and arranged functionally to conform to section configurations, include section descriptions and section drawing numbers in group drawing titles, such as "Section Through Building 1-A12."

TITLES FOR DRAWINGS AND DETAIL DRAWING SIZES   NTS

- See Chapter 6 for lettering height and vertical spacing for titles.
* See Schedule of Detail Drawing Sizes in Chapter 26 for recommended detail drawing sizes.

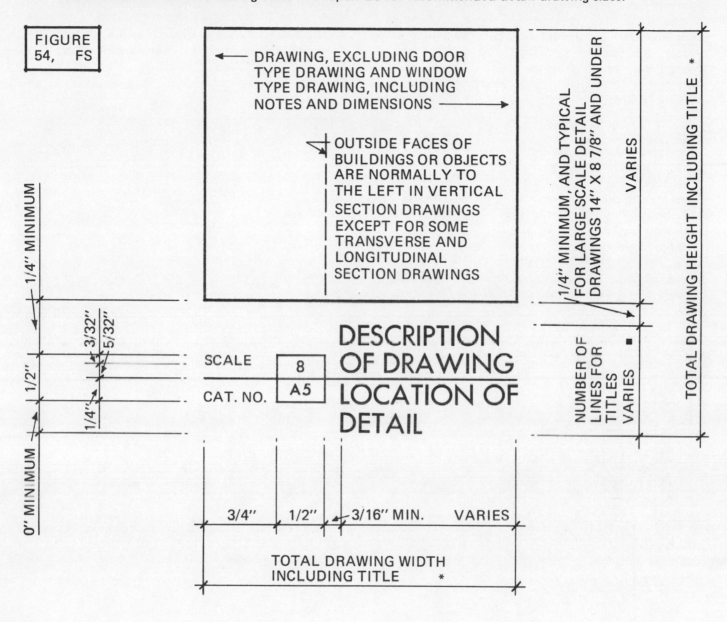

FIGURE 54, FS

DRAWING, EXCLUDING DOOR TYPE DRAWING AND WINDOW TYPE DRAWING, INCLUDING NOTES AND DIMENSIONS →

OUTSIDE FACES OF BUILDINGS OR OBJECTS ARE NORMALLY TO THE LEFT IN VERTICAL SECTION DRAWINGS EXCEPT FOR SOME TRANSVERSE AND LONGITUDINAL SECTION DRAWINGS

SCALE   8

CAT. NO.   A5

DESCRIPTION OF DRAWING LOCATION OF DETAIL

1/4" MINIMUM

3/32"
5/32"
1/4"

1/2"

0" MINIMUM

1/4" MINIMUM, AND TYPICAL FOR LARGE SCALE DETAIL DRAWINGS 14" X 8 7/8" AND UNDER

VARIES

NUMBER OF LINES FOR TITLES VARIES

TOTAL DRAWING HEIGHT INCLUDING TITLE   *

3/4"   1/2"   3/16" MIN.   VARIES

TOTAL DRAWING WIDTH INCLUDING TITLE   *

| 25 | **TECHNIQUES FOR PRE-SENTING ARCHITECTURAL DRAWINGS** | **LOCATIONS FOR REFERENCE SYMBOLS** | |

GENERAL

Reference symbols, that convey information directly and should be understandable to all members of the building industry, are shown and their contents explained in Chapter 18. The completed symbols are shown again in this chapter with directions for use in architectural working drawings. Use and locate the symbols on drawings as directed below.

DRAWING REFERENCE SYMBOL

Use the drawing reference symbol modified to reference drawings. Incorporate contents of the symbol; namely, drawing number and sheet number on which drawing is presented, in all Section Indication Symbols and in all Title Reference Symbols, except in door type, door frame detail, window type, and window detail title reference symbols.

DOOR REFERENCE SYMBOL

Use either door reference symbol-schedule method or door reference symbol-direct reference method to reference door frame and/or door information in a set of architectural working drawings. Where more detailed information is required, use the schedule method of door referencing. Where less detailed information is required, use the direct reference method of door referencing.

Place the door reference symbol in or near doorways on small scale floor plans only. For hinged, pivot, balanced, sliding, bi-fold, and folding doors, use the door reference symbol in doorways on small scale floor plans to reference door frame details. For all other doors, including rolling, overhead, vertical lift, and revolving doors, use the section cut symbol at doorways in exterior elevations and interior elevations to reference door frame details. For doors located in curtain walls, entrances, storefronts, or movable partitions, use the section cut symbol at doorways in exterior elevations, interior elevations, or detail elevations to reference door frame details.

WINDOW REFERENCE SYMBOL

Use the window reference symbol to reference window information. Place the symbol in or near punched opening windows on exterior elevations only. Do not use the symbol with curtain walls.

TITLE REFERENCE SYMBOL

Use the title reference symbol to reference drawings. Place the symbol under each drawing. List door types, door frame details, window types, and window details in list of drawings, since sheet numbers on which these drawings are presented are not contained in title reference symbols.

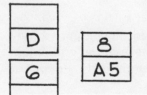

HALL
304

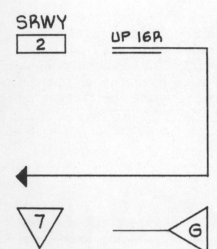

SRWY
2

UP 16R

7

G

L1

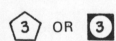

3 OR 3

127

ROOM REFERENCE SYMBOL

Use the room reference symbol to reference room information. Place the symbol in or near rooms on small scale floor plans, detail floor plans, finish flooring plans, and reflected ceiling plans. If required to clarify drawings, place the symbol without accompanying room name in rooms on small scale sections through building.

STAIRWAY REFERENCE SYMBOL AND STAIRS DIRECTION INDICATION

Use the stairway reference symbol and stairs direction indication to reference stair information and to show stairs direction. Place the symbol and indication in or near stairways on small scale floor plans, detail floor plans, and finish flooring plans. Place the symbol with accompanying name (SRWY) in or near stairways on reflected ceiling plans. If required to clarify drawings, place the symbol without accompanying name in stairways on small scale sections through building.

COLUMN LINE SYMBOL

Use column center lines, or more precisely, column reference lines, to reference columns. Show column reference lines and column line symbol with appropriate numbers or letters on plans, elevations, sections, and details.

ELEVATION MARK SYMBOL

Use the elevation mark symbol to designate critical reference or working points or levels. Place the elevation mark symbol on roof and floor dimension extension lines in exterior elevations, small scale sections through buildings, stair sections, roof-wall sections, floor-wall sections, roof sections, floor sections, wall vertical sections, and on site plans at floor level indications.

LOOSE LINTEL REFERENCE SYMBOL

Use the loose lintel reference symbol with the schedule-symbol method of loose lintel sizing. Place the symbol on small scale plans near lintels.

REVISION SYMBOL

Use the revision symbol on large-size working drawing sheets to identify revised drawing areas. Place the symbol on large-size working drawing sheets at revised drawing areas and in title blocks. Indicate all revision dates in title blocks on large-size working drawing sheets and the latest revision date in title blocks on small-size detail sheets. Do not erase previous revision symbols on drawings and in title blocks or previous revision dates in title blocks on large-size working drawing sheets.

EQUIPMENT SYMBOL

Use the equipment symbol to identify equipment, including cabinet-work, if required to clarify drawings. Place the symbol at equipment on plans, interior elevations, and details, if equipment numbering system is used.

DRAWING SIZES

To facilitate comprehension of drawings and to reduce production costs, prepare detail drawings to conform to uniform detail drawing sizes indicated in Schedule of Detail Drawing Sizes below.

SCHEDULE OF DETAIL DRAWING SIZES		
DETAIL DRAWING SIZE ■	TOTAL DRAW-ING WIDTH IN INCHES *	TOTAL DRAW-ING HEIGHT IN INCHES*
A	2	2 5/8
B	2	4 3/16
C	2	5 3/4
D	2	8 7/8
E	3 1/4	2 5/8
F	3 1/4	4 3/16
G	3 1/4	5 3/4
H	3 1/4	8 7/8
I	4 1/2	2 5/8
J	4 1/2	4 3/16
K	4 1/2	5 3/4
L	4 1/2	8 7/8
M	7	2 5/8
N	7	4 3/16
O	7	5 3/4
P	7	8 7/8
Q	8 7/8	7
R	14	8 7/8
S	8 7/8	14

■ Use these 19 uniform detail drawing sizes for detail drawings that measure 14" x 8 7/8" and under, if practical. Normal horizontal spacing and vertical spacing between detail drawings on small-size detail sheets is 1/2". The recommended detail drawing sizes permit several arrangements for detail drawings on small-size detail sheets.

* Total drawing width and total drawing height include drawing, notes, dimensions, title reference symbol, and title for drawing.

DRAWING ARRANGEMENTS

Drawing arrangements on large-size working drawing sheets and small-size detail sheets influence comprehension of design and construction information shown in drawings and affect production costs. To facilitate comprehension of drawings, group similar or related drawings in an orderly manner on one sheet; or, if this is impractical, group them on consecutive sheets. Position elevation and vertical section drawings on large-size working drawing sheets so that ground always faces bottoms of sheets. Orient small scale plans, and large scale plans if practical, always in the same direction (by pointing north arrows in sheet title blocks in one constant direction). Position small scale general drawing plans on sheets so that plans located on different sheets stack over each other in sets of drawings as building stories stack over each other in buildings. Cut all small scale and large scale vertical sections (except transverse and longitudinal sections through buildings or objects) clockwise so that outside faces of buildings or objects are to the left in drawings. Arrange detail drawings on large-size working drawing sheets and small-size detail sheets horizontally, vertically, functionally, or randomly. See Figure 55.

In Horizontal Detail Drawing Arrangements, a visible or invisible reference line, such as a column line, wall line, roof line, floor line, or ceiling line is established horizontally on a drawing sheet. Related detail drawings are grouped horizontally on the drawing sheet so that the horizontal reference line in each detail drawing coincides with the established horizontal reference line. Use this arrangement where the majority of detail drawings in a group relate to each other horizontally. Detail drawings normally arranged in this manner include Roof Sections, Floor Sections, Wall Plan Sections, Column Plan Sections, Detail Elevations, Window Types, Door Types, Threshold Details, Interior Elevations, Base Details, and Ceiling Details.

In Vertical Detail Drawing Arrangements, a visible or invisible reference line, such as a column line, wall line, door frame line, or window frame line is established vertically on a drawing sheet. Related detail drawings are grouped vertically on the drawing sheet so that the vertical reference line in each detail drawing coincides with the established vertical reference line. Use this arrangement where the majority of detail drawings in a group relate to each other vertically. Detail drawings normally arranged in this manner include Roof-Wall Sections, Floor-Wall Sections, Wall Vertical Sections, Entrance Details, Storefront Details, Window Details, Curtain Wall Details, Door Frame Details, Partition Details, Elevator Details, and Dumbwaiter Details.

In Functional Detail Drawing Arrangements, related horizontal or vertical section detail drawings are arranged on drawing sheets so that detail relationships and configurations of grouped details resemble imaginary or real small scale horizontal or vertical sections of objects detailed. In effect, functional detail drawing arrangements are large scale broken horizontal or vertical sections of buildings or objects. Detail drawings normally arranged in this manner include Building Construction vertical section Details (referenced from Small Scale Sections Through Building), Stair Details, Cabinetwork Details, and Escalator Details.

Grouping related detail drawings on drawing sheets in vertical and horizontal alignments to conform to predetermined configurations often results in unused areas on drawing sheets. These areas are not wasted because they are, in effect, integral parts of grouped drawings that permit configurations to be clearly expressed, facilitating comprehension of total design and construction. Groups of related detail drawings arranged functionally to conform to longitudinal and transverse sections cannot always include all vertical section detail drawings required to explain design and construction. Additional detail drawings are grouped in horizontal, vertical, or random drawing arrangements.

In Random Detail Drawing Arrangements, detail drawings are arbitrarily arranged on drawing sheets. Detail drawings normally arranged in this manner include Site Plan Details, Detail Plans, Detail Sections, Millwork Details, and Miscellaneous Details. Random detail drawing arrangements are normally used to present individual unrelated detail drawings, such as a single bench detail drawing, a single tackboard edge detail drawing, or a single skylight detail drawing. Random detail drawing arrangements may also be used to present, with more production efficiency and less contextual clarity, groups of related detail drawings, especially vertical section detail drawings that relate to each other vertically and horizontally. Detail drawings sometimes arranged in this manner include Building Construction vertical section Details (referenced from Small Scale Sections Through Building and other locations), Stair Details, Cabinetwork Details, and Escalator Details.

Reference building construction vertical section detail drawings from small scale sections through buildings using the section point symbol. Arrange the detail drawings randomly or functionally. Arrange building construction vertical section detail drawings not referenced from small scale sections through buildings randomly, horizontally, or vertically. The traditional "wall section" composed of full height combined roof-wall sections and floor-wall sections is seldom required in working drawings. On most building construction projects today, portions of walls between floors, or between roofs and floors, are architecturally uneventful and consequently do not require detailed graphic explanations in large scale vertical section detail drawings.

If isolation of individual detail drawings or isolation of groups of related detail drawings is required to improve comprehension of detail drawings, draw horizontal and vertical border lines between detail drawings so that each detail drawing or each group of related detail drawings is surrounded on all sides by sheet border lines and/or common detail border lines. If this bordering technique is used, use it consistently throughout the set of drawings.

ILLUSTRATION OF DRAWING ARRANGEMENTS

ON LARGE-SIZE WORKING DRAWING SHEET

NTS

ARRANGEMENTS FOR WINDOW AND DOOR FRAME DETAIL DRAWINGS

To facilitate comprehension of drawings and to reduce production costs, arrange window and door frame detail drawings on drawing sheets according to uniform arrangements shown in Figure 56. Window detail uniform drawing arrangements shown are for punched opening windows. Door frame detail uniform drawing arrangements shown are for hinged, pivot, balanced, sliding, bi-fold, and folding doors.

Use arrangements 3, 4, and 5 for windows. Use arrangements 1 and 2 for hinged, pivot, and balanced doors. Do not present threshold detail drawings for hinged, pivot, and balanced doors with door frame detail drawings. Use arrangement 2 for sliding, bi-fold, and folding doors that do not require sill detail drawings. Use arrangements 3 and 4 for sliding, bi-fold, and folding doors that require sill detail drawings. For hinged, pivot, and balanced doors, use arrangement 1 with direct reference method of door referencing and use arrangement 2 with schedule method of door referencing.

If individual window or door frame detail drawings cannot be limited to a 3 1/4" total drawing width, increase the width. If practical, include all window detail drawings pertaining to a particular punched opening window installation and all door frame detail drawings pertaining to a particular hinged, pivot, balanced, sliding, bi-fold, or folding door installation in a 7" wide by 8 7/8" high area, even if individual detail drawings do not conform to recommended detail drawing sizes.

If recommended uniform drawing arrangements shown in this chapter are inappropriate for a particular condition or a particular project, devise appropriate arrangements to suit condition or project.

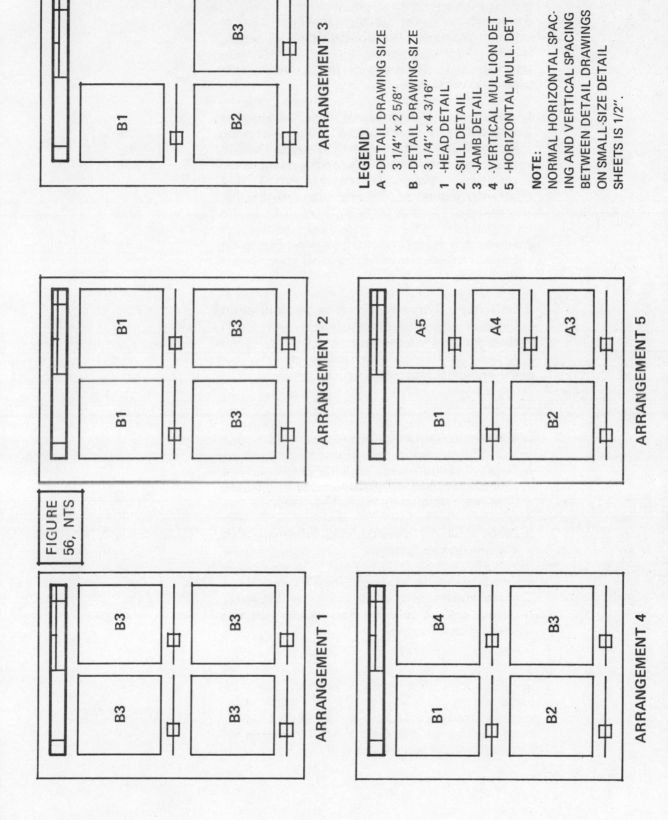

ARRANGEMENT 3

LEGEND

A - DETAIL DRAWING SIZE
    3 1/4" x 2 5/8"
B - DETAIL DRAWING SIZE
    3 1/4" x 4 3/16"
1 - HEAD DETAIL
2 - SILL DETAIL
3 - JAMB DETAIL
4 - VERTICAL MULLION DET
5 - HORIZONTAL MULL. DET

NOTE:
NORMAL HORIZONTAL SPAC-
ING AND VERTICAL SPACING
BETWEEN DETAIL DRAWINGS
ON SMALL-SIZE DETAIL
SHEETS IS 1/2".

ARRANGEMENT 2

ARRANGEMENT 5

FIGURE 56, NTS

ARRANGEMENT 1

ARRANGEMENT 4

NTS

ARRANGEMENTS FOR WINDOW AND DOOR FRAME DETAIL DRAWINGS

ON SMALL-SIZE DETAIL SHEET TYPE A

DRAWING PROCESS

Arrangements for Detail Drawings suggest systematic preparation of individual drawings. Normal drawing process for each architectural working drawing consists of the following nine chronological steps:

1. Medium and thin linework including site plan symbols and uncompleted Title Reference Symbol. Use medium lines for thick lines in this step. If thickness of linework is doubtful, use thin linework. Before drawing a detail drawing determine drawing size and title for drawing.

2. Dimension Lines and Dimension Extension Lines. Include dimensions in this step or in a later step.

3. Reference Symbols and Section Indication Symbols. Include information in symbols in this step or in a later step.

4. Material Indications in Section.

5. Notes.

6. Material Indications in Elevation.

7. Thick linework over medium linework (and thin linework) as required and medium linework over thin linework if required.

8. Scale, title for drawing, and information in Title Reference Symbol.

9. Check drawing content for accuracy and completeness and check drawing linework, notes, and dimensions for clarity. Correct drawing as required.

See page 5 for Office Architectural Drafting Standards and Symbols and page 77 for Project Architectural Drafting Standards and Symbols incorporated in drawings. See page 91 for Techniques for Presenting Architectural Drawings.

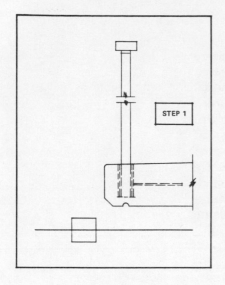

STEP 1

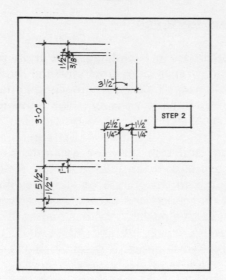

3'-0"

3½"

5½"

STEP 2

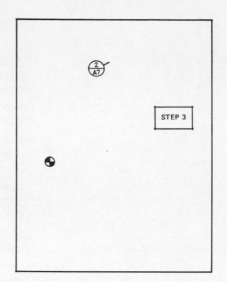

2
A7

STEP 3

½ FULL SIZE

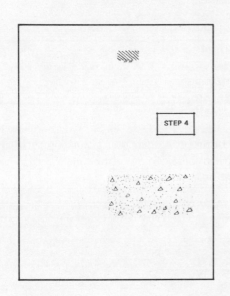

STEP 4

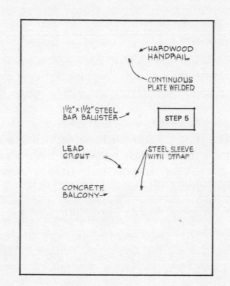

← HARDWOOD
HANDRAIL

CONTINUOUS
PLATE WELDED

1½" x 1½" STEEL
BAR BALUSTER

LEAD
GROUT

STEEL SLEEVE
WITH STRAP

CONCRETE
BALCONY

STEP 5

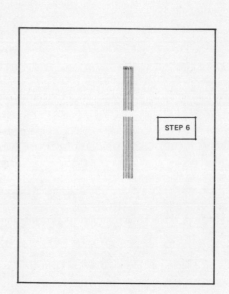

STEP 6

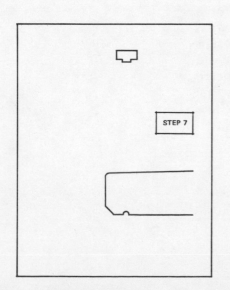

STEP 7

STEP 8

1½"=1'-0"   12   HANDRAIL DET
            A14   AT BALCONY

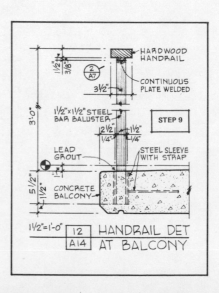

HARDWOOD
HANDRAIL

2
A7

CONTINUOUS
PLATE WELDED

3½"

3'-0"

1½" x 1½" STEEL
BAR BALUSTER

STEP 9

2½
¼"

1½"
¼"

LEAD
GROUT

STEEL SLEEVE
WITH STRAP

5½"

CONCRETE
BALCONY

1½"=1'-0"   12   HANDRAIL DET
            A14   AT BALCONY

SHEET LAYOUTS

Arrangements for Detail Drawings imply planning of production. Plan sets of working drawings to enhance comprehension of drawings on individual sheets, to provide continuity of drawings from sheet to sheet, and to estimate and control production costs. Before actual preparation of working drawings, list contents of the set of working drawings (on 8 ½" x 11" sheets of white paper) and indicate scale of each drawing listed. (For a checklist, see contents of Architectural Working Drawing Sections in Chapter 10.) Using this data, prepare (on individual 8 1/2" x 11" sheets of white paper, if possible) Sheet Layouts at 1/4 full size of each large-size working drawing sheet. Draw to scale simplified outlines of site plans, small scale plans, exterior elevations, small scale sections through buildings, and schedules on Sheet Layouts; label each outline. Allow space for notes, dimensions, and titles outside of outlines except for site plan outlines. Include space for notes, dimensions, and titles and indicate north arrows within site plan outlines. Indicate outlines of foundations in exterior elevations and small scale sections through buildings by continuous lines. Show first floor or main floor level on exterior elevations by dashed lines and on small scale sections through buildings by continuous lines. Estimate areas required for small scale and large scale detail drawings; label these undefined areas on Sheet Layouts. Estimate number of small-size detail sheets, if any.

Sheet Layouts are normally required for large projects, often required for medium projects, and sometimes required for small projects. Use Sheet Layouts to ascertain working drawing progress by comparing work actually completed on each working drawing sheet with work to be done, as shown on each corresponding Sheet Layout. Depending on size and complexity of project, working drawing progress is evaluated semimonthly or monthly. Sheet Layouts for a small building construction project are shown at 1/2 full size on following pages. The project is comparable in physical size and complexity to design projects in current examinations prepared by the National Council of Architectural Registration Boards and issued by State Architectural Registration Boards.

CONTENTS OF PLUMBING WORKING DRAWINGS

Foundation Plan - 1/8'' = 1'-0''
First Floor Plan - 1/8'' = 1'-0''
Second Floor Plan - 1/8'' = 1'-0''
Plumbing Details - scales as required

CONTENTS OF HEATING AND VENTILATION WORKING DRAWINGS

First Floor Plan - 1/8'' = 1'-0''
Furnace Room Plan - 1/2'' = 1'-0''
Furnace Room Section - 1/2'' = 1'-0''
Baseboard Diffuser Detail - 1 1/2'' = 1'-0''
Underfloor Duct Detail - 1 1/2'' = 1'-0''
Furnace Schedule
Air Cooled Condensing Unit Schedule
Grille and Diffuser Schedule
Miscellaneous Details - scales as required

CONTENTS OF ELECTRICAL WORKING DRAWINGS

First Floor Plan - 1/8'' = 1'-0''
Second Floor Plan - 1/8'' = 1'-0''
Lighting Fixture Schedule
Panel Schedule
One Line Distribution Diagram - NTS
Electrical Details - scales as required

SHEET LAYOUTS - CONTENTS OF WORKING DRAWINGS   JUNE 14, 1971
SAINT THOMAS CHURCH   PROJECT NO. 144-71

CONTENTS OF COMPOSITE WORKING DRAWINGS

List of Drawings
Project Drafting Standards and Symbols
Site Plan (A, S, P, H, E information) - 1'' = 10'-3''
Site Details - 3/4'' = 1'-0''

CONTENTS OF ARCHITECTURAL WORKING DRAWINGS

Foundation Plan - 1/8'' = 1'-0''
First Floor Plan - 1/8'' = 1'-0''
Second Floor Plan - 1/8'' = 1'-0''
Roof Plan - 1/16'' = 1'-0''
Equipment Plan - 1/8'' = 1'-0''
North Elevation - 1/8'' = 1'-0''
East Elevation - 1/8'' = 1'-0''
South Elevation - 1/8'' = 1'-0''
West Elevation - 1/8'' = 1'-0''
Longitudinal Section - 1/8'' = 1'-0''
Transverse Section - 1/8'' = 1'-0''
Building Construction Details - 1 1/2'' = 1'-0''
Interior Stair Section - 1/4'' = 1'-0''
Stair Details - 1 1/2'' = 1'-0''
Entrance Details - 1 1/2'' = 1'-0''
   Rooms 101, 106, 107.
Window Types - 1/4'' = 1'-0'' approximately
Window Details - 3'' = 1'-0''
Door Types - 1/4'' = 1'-0'' approximately
Door Frame Details - 3'' = 1'-0''
Interior Elevations - 1/4'' = 1'-0''
   Rooms, 101, 105, 108, 111, 112, 113, 114.
Detail Floor Plans - 1/4'' = 1'-0''
   Rooms 112, 113.
Cabinetwork Details - 1/4'' = 1'-0'' and 1 1/2'' = 1'-0''
Miscellaneous Details - scales as required
Room Finish Schedule (Q1002) - 19 rooms - 23 spaces min.
Door Schedule (Q1102) - 32 doors - 36 spaces min.

CONTENTS OF STRUCTURAL WORKING DRAWINGS

Foundation Plan - 1/8'' = 1'-0''
Foundation Details - 3/4'' = 1'-0''
Second Floor Framing Plan - 1/8'' = 1'-0''
Roof Framing Plan - 1/8'' = 1'-0''
Framing Details - 3/4'' = 1'-0''
Exterior Stair Section - 1/2'' = 1'-0''

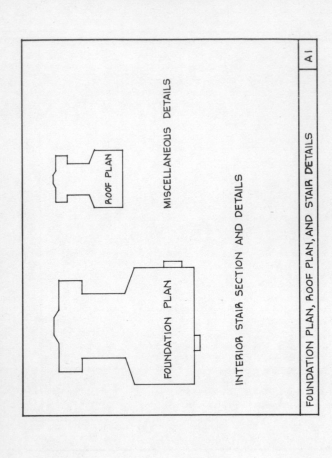

FOUNDATION PLAN, ROOF PLAN, AND STAIR DETAILS — A1

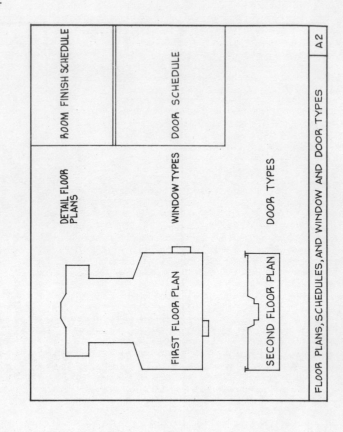

FLOOR PLANS, SCHEDULES, AND WINDOW AND DOOR TYPES — A2

LIST OF DRAWINGS

PROJECT DRAFTING STANDARDS AND SYMBOLS

TITLE SHEET — Z1

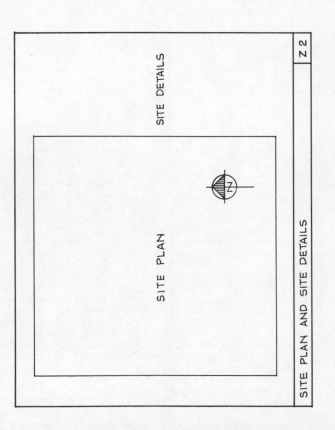

SITE PLAN AND SITE DETAILS — Z2

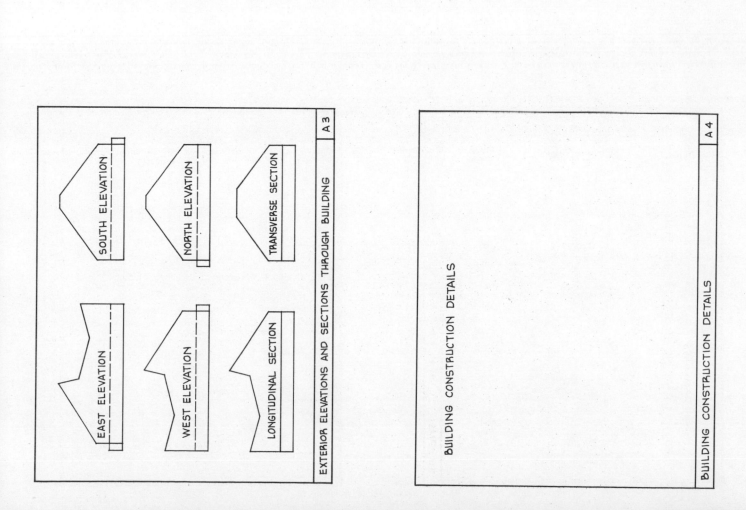

WINDOW DETAILS
DOOR FRAME DETAILS
ENTRANCE DETAILS

WINDOW, DOOR FRAME, AND ENTRANCE DETAILS

A 5

INTERIOR ELEVATIONS
CABINETWORK DETAILS

INTERIOR ELEVATIONS AND CABINETWORK DETAILS

A 6

SOUTH ELEVATION

NORTH ELEVATION

TRANSVERSE SECTION

EAST ELEVATION

WEST ELEVATION

LONGITUDINAL SECTION

EXTERIOR ELEVATIONS AND SECTIONS THROUGH BUILDING

A 3

BUILDING CONSTRUCTION DETAILS

BUILDING CONSTRUCTION DETAILS

A 4

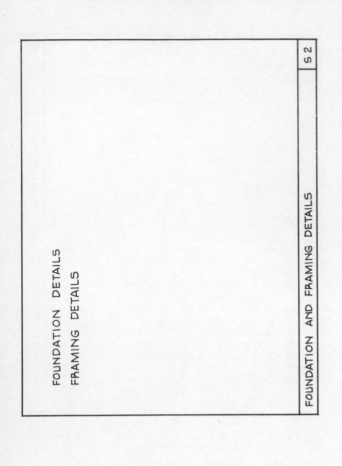

MISCELLANEOUS DETAILS

EQUIPMENT PLAN

A 7

EQUIPMENT PLAN AND MISCELLANEOUS DETAILS

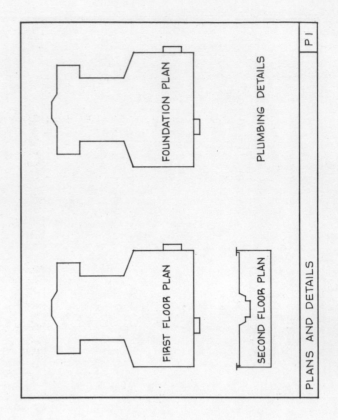

FOUNDATION PLAN

FIRST FLOOR PLAN

SECOND FLOOR PLAN

PLUMBING DETAILS

P I

PLANS AND DETAILS

FOUNDATION DETAILS

FRAMING DETAILS

S 2

FOUNDATION AND FRAMING DETAILS

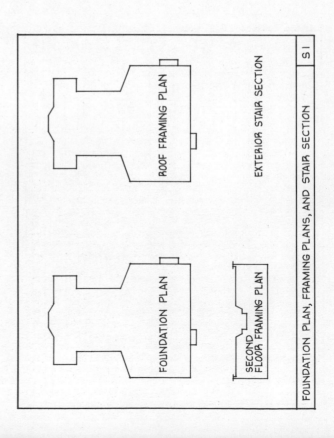

FOUNDATION PLAN

ROOF FRAMING PLAN

SECOND FLOOR FRAMING PLAN

EXTERIOR STAIR SECTION

S I

FOUNDATION PLAN, FRAMING PLANS, AND STAIR SECTION

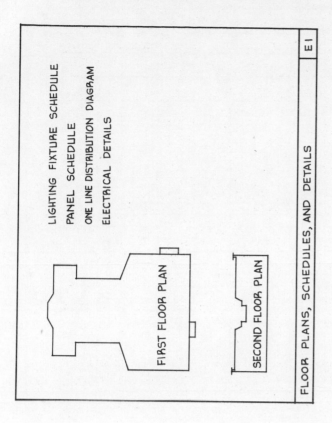

LIGHTING FIXTURE SCHEDULE
PANEL SCHEDULE
ONE LINE DISTRIBUTION DIAGRAM
ELECTRICAL DETAILS

FIRST FLOOR PLAN

SECOND FLOOR PLAN

E1

FLOOR PLANS, SCHEDULES, AND DETAILS

PLUMBING DETAILS

P 2

PLUMBING DETAILS

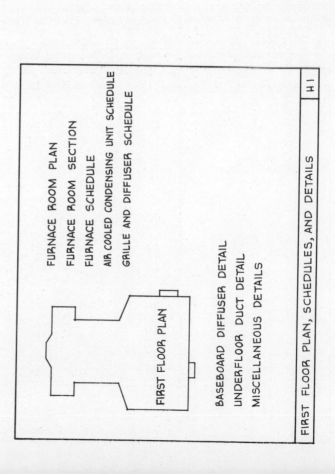

FURNACE ROOM PLAN
FURNACE ROOM SECTION
FURNACE SCHEDULE
AIR COOLED CONDENSING UNIT SCHEDULE
GRILLE AND DIFFUSER SCHEDULE

FIRST FLOOR PLAN

BASEBOARD DIFFUSER DETAIL
UNDERFLOOR DUCT DETAIL
MISCELLANEOUS DETAILS

H1

FIRST FLOOR PLAN, SCHEDULES, AND DETAILS

Completed Records of Original Working Drawings for a small building construction project are exhibited on this page to show how drawing progress can be ascertained by comparing copy of latest record with copy of previous record (or copies of previous records). See Chapter 12 for procedure for completing Record of Original Working Drawings Schedule Q10001.

GRAY & GREEN · ARCHITECTS
2607 OXFORD DRIVE
CHAMPAIGN, ILLINOIS 61820
SCHED Q10001 — PROJ. NO. 144-71 — DATE: 6-30-71 — SHT. NO. 1 OF 1
RECORD OF ORIGINAL WORKING DRAWINGS
WORKING DRAWING SHEET

NO.	STARTING DATE	ESTIMATED % COMPLETED	COMPLETION DATE	DRAFTSMAN	HOURS EST.	HOURS ACT.
Z1				W. JENKS	4	0
Z2	6-21-71		14	T. STEIN	28	16
A1	6-24-71		8	T. STEIN	28	8
A2	6-14-71		25	T. STEIN	36	28
A3	6-14-71		17	W. JENKS	28	18
A4	6-18-71		24	W. JENKS	48	24
A5				T. STEIN	32	0
A6				W. JENKS	28	0
A7				T. STEIN	20	0
S1	6-14-71		26	L. GAMBAIANI	32	24
S2	6-24-71		19	L. GAMBAIANI	32	20
P1					-	-
P2					-	-
H1					-	-
E1					-	-
		42%	133		316 100%	138 44%

GRAY & GREEN · ARCHITECTS
2607 OXFORD DRIVE
CHAMPAIGN, ILLINOIS 61820
SCHED Q10001 — PROJ. NO. 144-71 — DATE: 6-14-71 — SHT. NO. 1 OF 1
RECORD OF ORIGINAL WORKING DRAWINGS
WORKING DRAWING SHEET

NO.	STARTING DATE	ESTIMATED % COMPLETED	COMPLETION DATE	DRAFTSMAN	HOURS EST.	HOURS ACT.
Z1				W. JENKS	4	-
Z2				T. STEIN	28	-
A1				T. STEIN	28	-
A2	6-14-71			T. STEIN	36	-
A3	6-14-71			W. JENKS	28	-
A4				W. JENKS	48	-
A5				T. STEIN	32	-
A6				W. JENKS	28	-
A7				T. STEIN	20	-
S1	6-14-71			L. GAMBAIANI	32	-
S2				L. GAMBAIANI	32	-
P1					-	
P2					-	
H1					-	
E1					-	
		0%	0		316 100%	0 0%

Contents of Final Specifications for a small building construction project are exhibited on this page so that contents of final specifications can be compared with contents of working drawings shown on previous pages in this chapter. For a checklist of specification contents, see latest edition of The CSI Format for Construction Specifications.

CONTENTS OF FINAL SPECIFICATIONS
SAINT THOMAS CHURCH

JUNE 14, 1971
PROJECT NO. 144-71

REQUIREMENTS, FORMS, CONDITIONS

INSTRUCTIONS TO BIDDERS
FORM OF PROPOSAL
FORM OF AGREEMENT BETWEEN OWNER AND CONTRACTOR
STANDARD GENERAL CONDITIONS

SPECIFICATIONS

DIVISION 1 – GENERAL REQUIREMENTS
    Section 1A – Summary of the Work
    Section 1B – Cash Allowances
    Section 1C – Alternates

DIVISION 2 – SITE WORK
    Section 2A – Site Work

DIVISION 3 – CONCRETE
    Section 3A – Concrete Work

DIVISION 4 – MASONRY
    Section 4A – Masonry Work

DIVISION 5 – METALS
    Section 5A – Structural and Miscellaneous Metal

DIVISION 6 – WOOD AND PLASTICS
    Section 6A – Carpentry and Millwork
    Section 6B – Drywall Construction
    Section 6C – Laminated Wood Beams and Columns
    Section 6D – Laminated Wood Roof Deck

DIVISION 7 – THERMAL AND MOISTURE PROTECTION
    Section 7A – Roofing, Sheet Metal, Caulking

DIVISION 8 – DOORS AND WINDOWS
    Section 8A – Doors
    Section 8B – Windows, Glass, and Glazing

DIVISION 9 – FINISHES
    Section 9A – Resilient Flooring
    Section 9B – Painting and Finishing

DIVISION 10 – SPECIALTIES – VOID

DIVISION 11 – EQUIPMENT – VOID

DIVISION 12 – FURNISHINGS – VOID

DIVISION 13 – SPECIAL CONSTRUCTION – VOID

DIVISION 14 – CONVEYING SYSTEMS – VOID

DIVISION 15 – MECHANICAL
    Section 15A – Plumbing Work
    Section 15B – Heating and Ventilation Work

DIVISION 16 – ELECTRICAL
    Section 16A – Electrical Work

A final specification section for a small building construction project and a related working drawing are exhibited on this page to show the relationship between specifications and drawings, to show how a specification that calls for shop drawings can reduce the number of working drawings and the amount of information contained in them,

and to show that many words and a few drawings can often convey required design and construction information more concisely and more economically than many drawings and a few words. For a specification section format for medium and large projects, see latest edition of The CSI Section Format.

SECTION 6C – LAMINATED WOOD BEAMS AND COLUMNS   6C1
PROJECT NO. 144-71   SAINT THOMAS CHURCH, MORANVILLE, ILLINOIS

PART 1: GENERAL

6C-01 GENERAL NOTES:

Standard General Conditions and Specification Division 1 – General Requirements apply to all work in this section. For locations and graphic explanations of work, see drawings, in particular, drawings 2–S1 and 3–S1.

6C-02 SHOP DRAWINGS:

The fabricator shall furnish complete shop drawings showing all details required for fabrication and installation of laminated members in accordance with Article 4.13 of the General Conditions. See drawing 8–S2 for typical beam end and bearing plate detail. Installation drawings shall show bearing plates with sizes and elevations noted. Hardware required for assembly and connection of members shall also be shown and sized on shop drawings. Contractor shall verify all dimensions at building site.

PART 2: PRODUCTS

6C-03 LUMBER AND ADHESIVES:

Laminated lumber shall be kiln-dried Coast region Douglas fir or Pine meeting the structural requirements of CS 253-63 and applicable local Codes. Lumber shall be of such stress grade as to provide glued laminated members with normal working stress values of 165 psi in shear parallel to grain, 1,800,000 psi in modulus of elasticity, 2400 psi in bending, 2400 psi in tension, and 1900 psi in compression parallel to grain. Waterproof adhesive conforming to Military Specification MIL-A-397B shall be used.

6C-04 APPEARANCE GRADE AND FINISH AND WRAPPING:

Appearance of members shall be Premium Grade as defined in the Standard Appearance Grades for Structural Glued Laminated Timber, AITC 110. Exposed faces of members shall be factory-applied stain and varnish as selected by the architect. Ends of laminated wood beams exposed to the weather shall be pressure treated with Cellon. Provide water-resistant reinforced kraft paper protective wrapping covering all surfaces of each individual member.

6C-05 HARDWARE:

The fabricator shall furnish all metal shapes for joining laminated members to each other and/or to their supports, except for anchor bolts embedded in masonry, tie rods, bearing plates or items welded to structural steel.

6C-06 MANUFACTURE:

Manufacture of structural glued laminated timber shall be by a qualified fabricator and shall conform to the U. S. Department of Commerce Commercial Standard CS 253-63 for Structural Glued Laminated Timber (effective April 1, 1963) and the American Institute of Timber Construction Standards, AITC 100.

SECTION 6C – PROJECT NO. 144-71   6C2

6C-07 QUALITY CONTROL:

Quality control shall be provided in accordance with CS 253-63, the Commercial Standard for Structural Glued Laminated Timber, and the American Institute of Timber Construction Inspection Manual, AITC 200. A Certificate of Conformance to these requirements shall be furnished and the AITC Quality Mark shall appear on all members.

PART 3: EXECUTION

6C-08 STORAGE AND ERECTION:

The general contractor is responsible for protection of the materials at all times after arrival at destination by rail car or truck. If stored temporarily, members shall be placed on blocks well off the ground and separated with wood strips so that air can circulate around each member. Top and sides of stored material shall be covered with moisture resistant paper. Nonmarring slings shall be used when handling. Roof sheathing shall be applied soon after erection. Protective wrapping shall remain on the members until they are enclosed within the building. Initial building heat shall be elevated gradually to the desired level. To minimize surface checking, the building relative humidity shall not be reduced rapidly.

Laminated wood beam and column installations shall conform to recommended best practices by beam and column manufacturer.

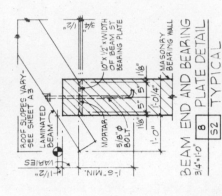

BEAM END AND BEARING PLATE DETAIL
8 S2 TYPICAL
3/4"=1'-0"

Schematic Design Outline Specifications (sometimes called Preliminary Outline Specifications) for a small building construction project are exhibited on this page to show the difference between nontechnical outline specifications and a technical final specification section shown on the previous page.

SCHEMATIC DESIGN OUTLINE SPECIFICATIONS   MAY 12, 1971
PROPOSED SAINT THOMAS CHURCH   MORANVILLE, ILLINOIS
GRAY AND GREEN - ARCHITECTS   2607 OXFORD DRIVE, CHAMPAIGN, ILLINOIS

1. BUILDING CODE OCCUPANCY CLASSIFICATION: Church - Group F-4.

2. BUILDING CODE CONSTRUCTION TYPE: 3A-Exterior Masonry Walls, Heavy Timbers (Mill).

3. FOUNDATIONS: Spread concrete footings; concrete foundation walls; sand fill and moisture barrier under all concrete floor slabs on grade; no footing drainage.

4. STRUCTURAL SYSTEMS AND MATERIALS: Masonry bearing walls; laminated wood beams; laminated wood roof deck.

5. FLOOR FRAMING: Concrete slab on grade; laminated wood beams with 3" wood subfloor and 1" wood finish floor.

6. FINISH FLOORING: Vinyl asbestos - typical; hardwood at Sanctuary platform for stain and varnish; exposed aggregate concrete slabs at Narthex-Baptistry and main entrance closet.

7. STAIRS: Folding wood.

8. ROOF FRAMING: Laminated wood beams and laminated wood deck for stain and varnish; rigid insulation on roof deck.

9. ROOFING: Asphalt shingles; copper flashing; copper roof gutters at main entrance portico roofs with copper leaders to splash blocks.

10. EXTERIOR WALLS: Common bond face brick solid bearing walls.

11. WINDOWS: Wood frames; wood operating sashes at south wall; clear glass - typical; obscure colored glass at Baptistry, Chapel, and Sanctuary skylight; all wood for stain and varnish.

12. EXTERIOR DOORS AND FRAMES: Solid core wood doors; wood frames; all wood for stain and varnish.

13. INTERIOR PARTITIONS: Brick; concrete block for paint.

14. INTERIOR DOORS AND FRAMES: Hollow core wood doors; wood frames - typical; all wood for stain and varnish.

15. BASES: Brick; topset vinyl.

16. INTERIOR TRIM: Wood for stain and varnish.

17. CEILINGS: Wood deck for stain and varnish; acoustic tile at Confessional, main entrance storage and closet, and Priests' Sacristy.

18. FIREPROOFING: None.

19. MILLWORK AND CABINET WORK: Wood Sacristy cabinets for stain and varnish.

20. SITE IMPROVEMENTS: Exposed aggregate concrete Atrium; broom finish concrete walks.

21. PLUMBING: City water supply; gas water heater; sanitary sewage to city sanitary sewer; storm sewage system not required.

22. HEATING AND VENTILATION: Forced warm and cold air for winter heating and summer cooling; gas-fired furnaces; air cooled condensing units.

23. ELECTRICAL: Underground electric service; incandescent and fluorescent lighting; wall mounted lighting fixtures typical in public spaces.

24. ITEMS NOT IN CONTRACT: Nave seating, organ, confessional furniture and curtain, mass schedule sign, altar, two standing processional candlesticks, processional cross, ambo, three chairs, credence, ambry, tabernacle, sanctuary lamp, baptismal font, baptismal cabinet, baptismal font cover, paschal candlestick, and stations of the cross.

A TECHNIQUE FOR PRESENTING DETAIL DRAWINGS

In Chapter 1 it was asserted that a standard format for working drawings would allow detail drawings in files, catalogs, electronic film readers, and computers to be directly incorporated into working drawings. An inevitable procedure for collating and presenting detail drawings that conform to the standard format for architectural working drawings in this book is outlined below.

1. Examine detail drawings in old catalogs.

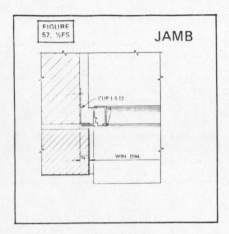

2. Examine detail drawings in new catalogs, files, electronic film readers, and computers.

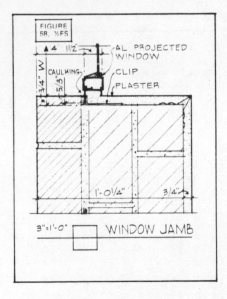

3. Evaluate detail drawings presented and select appropriate detail drawings and/or prepare appropriate detail drawings.

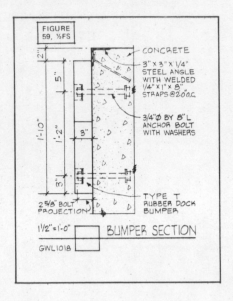

4. Delete unnecessary or inapplicable information from originals and/or copies of detail drawings. Add specific title information, and other information if required or desired.

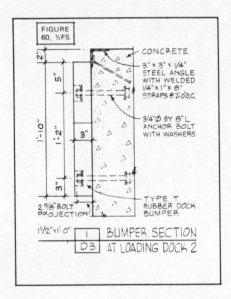

5. Cut, arrange, and paste originals and/or copies of detail drawings on standard drawing sheets for reproduction. See Figure 61 on next page.

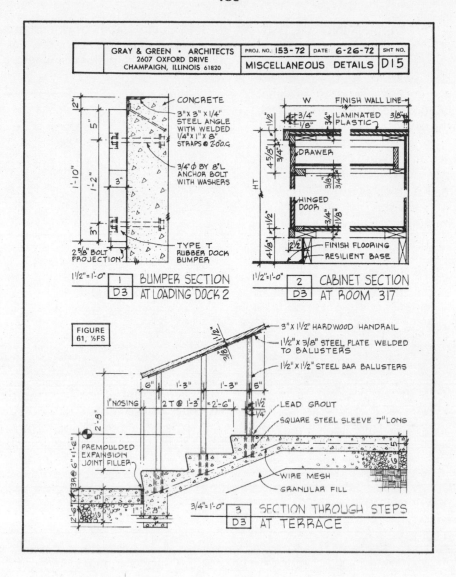

GRAY & GREEN · ARCHITECTS
2607 OXFORD DRIVE
CHAMPAIGN, ILLINOIS 61820

PROJ. NO.: 153-72 DATE: 6-26-72 SHT NO.

MISCELLANEOUS DETAILS D15

CONCRETE

3"x 3" x 1/4"
STEEL ANGLE
WITH WELDED
1/4"x 1"x 8"
STRAPS @ 2'-0"O.C.

3/4" Ø BY 8"L
ANCHOR BOLT
WITH WASHERS

TYPE T
RUBBER DOCK
BUMPER

2 5/8" BOLT
PROJECTION

1 1/2"=1'-0"   1   BUMPER SECTION
               D3 AT LOADING DOCK 2

W   FINISH WALL LINE
LAMINATED
PLASTIC
DRAWER
HINGED DOOR
FINISH FLOORING
RESILIENT BASE

1 1/2"=1'-0"   2   CABINET SECTION
               D3 AT ROOM 317

FIGURE 61, 1/2FS

3"x 1 1/2" HARDWOOD HANDRAIL
1 1/2" x 3/8" STEEL PLATE WELDED TO BALUSTERS
1 1/2" x 1 1/2" STEEL BAR BALUSTERS
LEAD GROUT
SQUARE STEEL SLEEVE 7" LONG

1" NOSING   2 T @ 1'-3" = 2'-6"

PREMOULDED
EXPANSION
JOINT FILLER

WIRE MESH
GRANULAR FILL

3/4"=1'-0"   3   SECTION THROUGH STEPS
             D3 AT TERRACE

| 27 | TECHNIQUES FOR PRE-SENTING ARCHITECTURAL DRAWINGS | MISCELLANEOUS TECHNIQUES FOR PRESENTING DRAWINGS | |

Formulate additional techniques for presenting drawings, if required. Devise them to complement techniques outlined in Chapters 23 through 26.

GRAPHIC COMMUNICATIONS IN ARCHITECTURE	INDICES

SUBJECT INDEX

DRAWING INDEX

EXAMPLES OF BASIC ARCHITECTURAL WORKING DRAWINGS

EVALUATION OF ARCHITECTURAL WORKING DRAWING SHEETS

Sheet Composition - 10%
1. Clarity of presentation, 130-133, 139.
2. detail drawing sizes, 121.
3. detail drawing arrangements (horizontal, vertical, functional, random), 123, 125.
4. small scale general drawing placements, 121.
5. completion of title block, 73.

Linework - 10%
1. Line widths (extra thick, thick, medium, thin), 17.
2. line types (dotted, short dashed, long dashed, extra long dashed, continuous, combinations), 17-19.
3. sharpness, denseness, width uniformity, value consistency, 17-19.
4. material indications in section, 81-82.
5. material indications in elevation, 25-26.
6. site plan symbols, 79-80.
7. reference symbols, 83-84, 117-118.
8. section indication symbols, 39-40.
9. title reference symbol, 40, 83, 115, 117.
10. comprehensibility, 17-21, 126-127.

Lettering - 10%
1. heights (3/16", 1/8", 3/32"), 23.
2. vertical spacings (1/8", 1/16"), 23.
3. horizontal spacings (1/32" minimum), 23.
4. minimum thickness (medium line width), 23.
5. style, consistency, and readability, 23-24.

Notes and Dimensions - 10%
1. notes: relevancy, correctness, quantity, placement, vertical alignment; correctness of information in title reference symbols; correctness of drawing titles; see pages 111-115 and 126-127.
2. dimensions: relevancy, correctness, quantity, placement, dimension lines, and dimension extension lines; see pages 85, 93-109, and 126-127.

Drawing Contents or Problem Solution - 60%
1. varies with each sheet or problem.

STANDARD FORMAT MATERIAL

To reduce drafting time and to facilitate a uniform approach to working drawings, material pertaining to the standard format for working drawings in this book is available commercially. Material consists of 8½" x 11" pad of *Project Architectural Drafting Standards and Symbols, and Schedules* shown in Chapters 16, 17, 18, 19, 20, and 12, and 4½" x 3¼" plastic *Symbols Template and Lettering Guide.* The pad containing 27 pages may be purchased from Stipes Publishing Company, 10 Chester Street, Champaign, Illinois 61820. The template along with circle and plumbing fixture templates are normally the only templates required in the preparation of architectural working drawings. The template (No. 1001) with 49 holes for drawing guidelines and 19 cutouts for drawing 26 different architectural drafting symbols may be purchased from Unifier Templates, P.O. Box 1151, Champaign, Illinois 61820. An illustration of the template and architectural drafting symbols constructed with the aid of the template are shown below. Order forms for book and pad and for template are printed on the next sheet. Large-size working drawing sheets and small-size detail sheets shown in Chapter 13 are not available at this time.

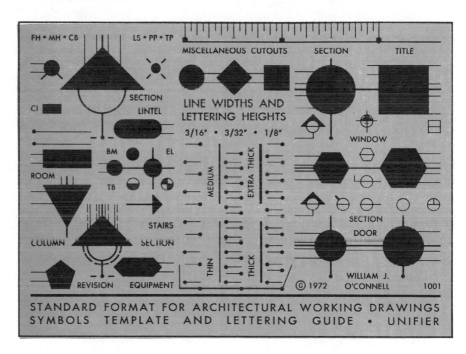

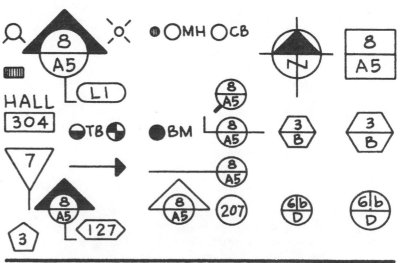

ARCHITECTURAL DRAFTING SYMBOLS

ORDER FORMS

BOOK AND PAD

GRAPHIC COMMUNICATIONS IN ARCHITECTURE • O'CONNELL 1974

BOOK PRICE IS $6.00 AND PAD PRICE IS $1.00. ENCLOSE CHECK WITH ORDER. MAKE CHECK PAYABLE TO STIPES PUBLISHING CO. PUBLISHER WILL PAY MAILING COSTS IN U.S.A. & CANADA.

NAME _____

ADDRESS _____

CITY _____

STATE _____ ZIP _____

NO./BOOKS _____ @ $6.00 AMOUNT $ _____

NO./PADS _____ @ $1.00 AMOUNT $ _____

TOTAL AMOUNT OF ORDER $ _____

STIPES PUBLISHING COMPANY
10 CHESTER ST. • CHAMPAIGN, IL 61820

TEMPLATE

SYMBOLS TEMPLATE AND LETTERING GUIDE • O'CONNELL 1974

TEMPLATE 1001 PRICE IS $2.50. ENCLOSE CHECK WITH ORDER. MAKE CHECK PAYABLE TO UNIFIER TEMPLATES. MAILING COSTS ARE INCLUDED IN TEMPLATE PRICE.

NAME _____

ADDRESS _____

CITY _____

STATE _____ ZIP _____

NUMBER OF TEMPLATES _____ @ $2.50 AMOUNT $ _____

UNIFIER TEMPLATES
P. O. BOX 1151 • CHAMPAIGN, IL 61820

GRAPHIC COMMUNICATIONS IN ARCHITECTURE • O'CONNELL 1974

BOOK PRICE IS $6.00 AND PAD PRICE IS $1.00. ENCLOSE CHECK WITH ORDER. MAKE CHECK PAYABLE TO STIPES PUBLISHING CO. PUBLISHER WILL PAY MAILING COSTS IN U.S.A. & CANADA.

NAME _____

ADDRESS _____

CITY _____

STATE _____ ZIP _____

NO./BOOKS _____ @ $6.00 AMOUNT $ _____

NO./PADS _____ @ $1.00 AMOUNT $ _____

TOTAL AMOUNT OF ORDER $ _____

STIPES PUBLISHING COMPANY
10 CHESTER ST. • CHAMPAIGN, IL 61820

SYMBOLS TEMPLATE AND LETTERING GUIDE • O'CONNELL 1974

TEMPLATE 1001 PRICE IS $2.50. ENCLOSE CHECK WITH ORDER. MAKE CHECK PAYABLE TO UNIFIER TEMPLATES. MAILING COSTS ARE INCLUDED IN TEMPLATE PRICE.

NAME _____

ADDRESS _____

CITY _____

STATE _____ ZIP _____

NUMBER OF TEMPLATES _____ @ $2.50 AMOUNT $ _____

UNIFIER TEMPLATES
P. O. BOX 1151 • CHAMPAIGN, IL 61820